BLENDER 4.3
USER GUIDE

A Comprehensive Guide to Animation
and Modeling

BEN TAYLOR

TABLE OF CONTENTS

CHAPTER ONE

INTRODUCTION

Overview of Blender 4.3

Blender 4.3 provides several core enhancements that enhance the operational capabilities of creative workers along with animation experts as well as the development community. Blender 4.3 delivers its main features which include:

1. User Interface Enhancements

- **More Customization**: Workspaces and toolbars and editor layouts in Blender received better customization tools which help users better match their workflow needs.
- **Streamlined Workflow**: Blender 4.3 provides users with an improved workflow design which simplifies access to essential tools for better operational performance.

2. Modeling Improvements

- **Sculpting Enhancements**: The sculpting abilities got better after receiving updated brushes and enhanced symmetry tools and advanced mesh management features to provide users with more power while sculpting.

- **Mesh Modeling Tools**: The modeling tools now include improved geometry processing while being enriched with better mesh cleanup tools and an enhanced Boolean operations function.

3. Animation and Rigging Tools

- **Overhauled Animation System**: The animation system now provides new management features for keyframes through an enhanced graph editor alongside a larger pose library system that helps animators.
- **Advanced Rigging**: The functionality in Advanced Rigging enables users to create easier character and item rigs because it provides enhanced skinning methods combined with automatic rig generation tools.

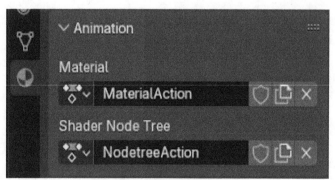

Animation & Rigging

4. Rendering and Visual Effects

- **Cycles and Eevee Upgrades**: The recent update of version 4.3 allows Cycles to handle rendering more efficiently through faster execution and additional denoising capabilities and better light scattering functions. Eevee updated its features to add realistic real-time rendering functions which operate within the application.

Cycles and Eevee Upgrades

- **Better Performance**: The application delivers enhanced viewport visualization with reduced time delays combined with increased rendering speed for instant final rendering results.

5. Simulation Tools

- **Fluid and Smoke Simulations**: The simulation systems for fluid and smoke now generate improved results through improved processing efficiency to create stable results.

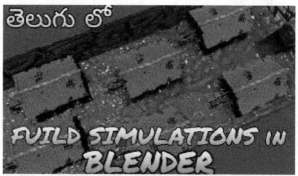
Fluid Simulations in Blender

- **Cloth and Hair Improvements**: Through its framework users can improve their cloth and hair modeling and operations to enhance animation rendering results.

6. Grease Pencil

- **2D and 3D Workflow Integration**: The animation software gives users new Grease Pencil capabilities which let them combine 2D drawing with 3D models to achieve more sophisticated storytelling features.

Grease Pencil

7. Python API and Scripting

- **Expanded API**: The Python API increased its scope to give users more control features which allow automated operations for multiple Blender internal systems.

- **New Add-ons**: The platform features several new add-ons that simplify operations while adding extra functionality from other software programs in Blender version 4.3.

Python API and Scripting

8. Performance and Collaboration

- **Faster Performance**: The program performance in Blender Version 4.3 demonstrates optimized thread handling and streamlined memory management which delivers faster system operation across all computers.
- **Collaboration Tools**: Blender 4.3 brings together two new collaboration tools that provide both an asset browser and team workflows which enhance group project work.

The new version of Blender 4.3 delivers both innovative working procedures and sophisticated advanced tools which build upon the previous version features. Due to market demand the software serves as a top solution for professional users in 3D content creation.

New Features and Improvements

The latest features in Blender 4.3 strengthen different software components to establish the tool as an effective platform for generating three-dimensional content. Users will benefit from significant updates found in this software version:

1. User Interface (UI) Updates

- **Custom Workspaces**: Each user gains customizable workspaces through which they can customize workspace structures to match their individual requirements. Users can customize their work tools in Blender by adding customized toolbars while also adjusting the positions of all interface editors.

- **Enhanced Tooltips & Icons**: Tooltips and icons have received an improvement through the software by offering tool description details in straightforward descriptions. The application updated several icons for better usability.

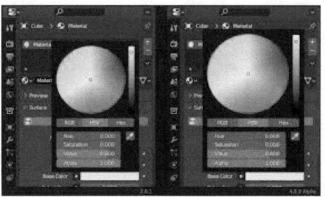
User Interface (UI) Updates

2. Modeling Enhancements

- **New Geometry Nodes Features**: The Geometry Nodes received new capabilities through union tools that boost procedural modeling possibilities through advanced mesh control methods and attribute improvement nodes.

- **Boolean Operations**: Boolean Operations achieved enhanced performance refinements through the combination of quicker speed with improved management features for complicated layout designs.

- **Mesh Cleanup Tools**: The automatic update provided Mesh Cleanup Tools with capabilities that simplified mesh repairs and sped up time for mesh resolution.

3. Sculpting Tools

- **Advanced Brushes**: The Blender 4.3 software brings customized advanced sculpting brushes to users for improved surface texture manipulation during work.

- **Multiresolution Improvements**: Users experience expedited operations of the multiresolution modifier while it handles complex and extensive meshes.

- **Enhanced Symmetry**: The software now provides better control over detailed mirroring features because its symmetrical tools received enhancements.

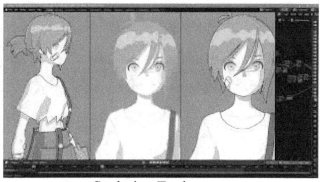
Sculpting Tools

4. Animation & Rigging

- **New Animation Layers**: Users obtain non-invasive animation functions with the addition of New

Animation Layers to Blender 4.3. The animation industry now uses simplified methods that allow animators to merge several animations together for complete production results.

- **Auto-Rigging and Retargeting**: The software gained improvements in auto-rigging functionality and developers created a tool to help users easily perform rig retargeting operations.
- **Pose Library Enhancements**: The new pose library enables users to optimize their pose handling thus improving object and character pose management.

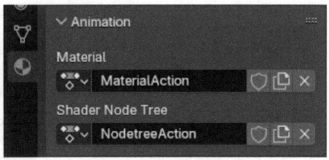
Animation & Rigging

5. Rendering Enhancements

- **Faster Cycles Rendering**: The performance of Cycles rendering enhancements have surged because the software supports faster GPUs and

14

implements efficient denoising mechanisms and completes light path calculations more quickly to deliver faster rendering times.

Faster Cycles Rendering

- **Eevee Improvements**: An upgrade to Eevee real-time performance happened when developers enhanced its reflective abilities and light rendering techniques and implemented subsurface scattering methods to achieve realistic materials.
- **Path Tracing in Eevee**: The experimental Path Tracing feature of Eevee enables users to conduct basic path tracing operations resulting in real-time preview outputs that approach Cycles rendering quality.

6. Simulation Updates

- **Cloth Simulation**: The updated cloth simulation capabilities result in stable fabric behavior and genuine simulation results for both cloth and soft materials during the process.

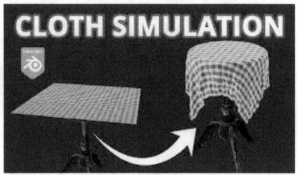
Cloth Simulation

- **Rigid Body Physics**: Better collision detection mechanisms have improved rigid body simulation operations as well as rapid performance improvements occur when dealing with complex setup models.

Rigid Body Physics

- **Fluid and Smoke Simulations**: The latest experimental function within Eevee enables basic path tracing for real-time preview that reaches nearly identical outcomes to Cycles rendering quality.

7. Grease Pencil and 2D Animation

- **Improved 3D to 2D Workflow**: Blender 4.3 improves functionality between combining 3D objects and 2D Grease Pencil environments thus enabling better storytelling options and animation development.
- **Advanced Drawing Tools**: Advanced Drawing Tools now come with Grease Pencil brushes in combination with layers to help artists improve

conceptual artwork production as well as develop their drawing techniques for better 2D animation.

Grease Pencil 2D

8. Python API & Scripting

- **Extended API**: The Python API received expanded internal system access through its extended capabilities so developers can create efficient process automations and advanced add-on frameworks.

- **New Add-ons**: The update package contains multiple built-in add-ons that make basic operations easier for users and create linkages between third-party programs and expand Blender's functionality.

9. Asset Browser & Collaboration

- **Asset Management System**: The Asset Management System within Blender 4.3 enhances functionality by delivering an upgraded Asset Browser that improves project-based asset reuse for materials and models as well as textures.

- **Team Collaboration Tools**: The new team collaboration tools contain advanced version control functionality as well as simpler asset sharing options that also present user-friendly management interfaces for team workflows.

10. Performance Optimizations

- **Viewport Performance**: The optimized viewport enhances viewport navigation along with better control of complex scenes while demanding high-poly models.
- **Memory Usage**: System users achieve better memory performance because the updated system allocates less memory which leads to larger project capacities without experiencing performance difficulties.

Blender 4.3 provides improved capabilities at the same time as improved usability and friendliness which enhances the workflow for individual artists and collaboration teams producing professional three-dimensional content at higher speeds.

CHAPTER TWO

MODELING

Enhanced Sculpting Tools

Multi-tool sculpting features found in Blender version 4.3 present better speed and heightened exactness during all sculpting tasks. The software developers integrated functional updates into the system to enable users better access intuitive features which create improved design details with flexible control systems. The major enhancements of Blender 4.3 for sculpting features consist of the following components:

1. New Brushes and Stroke Options

- **Advanced Brush Settings**: The 4.3 version of Blender features advanced brush settings that boost user control during brush operation. Using enhanced parameters representation enables users to shape and control design parameters better for producing complex detailed surfaces.

- **Dynamic Brush Textures**: The release brings Dynamic Brush Textures which automatically alter brush behavior based on current sculpted surface features. When traveling across surface details the brush will transform its density and shape characteristics automatically to create authentic natural brush mark sequences.

- **Multi-Shape Brushes**: The latest Blender 4.3 software release provides brushes that unite multiple shapes to create highly detailed sculpting functions. Various multilayered effects are achievable with these brushes which let users paint complex details such as wrinkles pores and fabric textures through a single brushstroke.

2. Sculpting Performance Improvements

- **Faster Multiresolution Sculpting**: Users experience fast Multiresolution Sculpting because the Multiresolution Modifier operates at impressive speeds even during high-resolution details work. Users can process dense meshes having numerous polygons due to upgraded system performance.
- **Better Performance with High-Poly Meshes**: High-poly mesh operation becomes more comfortable for artists during sculpting sessions. Big meshes in Blender 4.3 perform better thereby enhancing the sculpt functions especially for detailed character and object work with million vertex meshes.

- **Dynamic Tesselation**: Blendertreels new version implements built-in automatic mesh resolution improvement through dynamic tesselation features that operate in detail-relevant zones. By refining mesh details in precise regions sculptors can work on essential areas without causing any negative effects on system performance.

Dynamic Tessellation

3. Improved Symmetry and Asymmetry Tools

- **Advanced Symmetry Options**: Advanced Symmetry Options represent one of the many new features Blender 4.3 introduced for sculpting objects with symmetry. The new update allows users to set up asymmetric sculpting by selecting specific axes along with regions they want to receive asymmetrical intervention. The tool enables users to generate objects needing irregular marks

22

alongside various irregular shapes through its featured functions.

- **Local Symmetry**: Users can enable symmetry on chosen mesh parts when they work on specific mesh areas. Through the tool system users generate symmetrical areas which enable them to operate separately on different sections of their models.

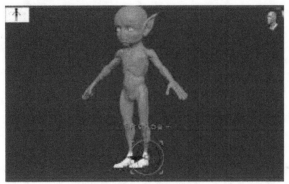

Local Symmetry

4. New Smoothing and Refining Tools

- **Sculpt Smooth Brush**: The Sculpt Smooth Brush delivers upgraded control to users who need to smooth model surfaces. The new tool delivers natural smoothing functions to users without compromising details because it includes adjustable control options.

- **Detail Enhancer**: Users can benefit from Detail Enhancer because the tool lets them refine and define model details through mesh adjustments that do not result in noticeable mesh distortion. The tool delivers essential advantages for enhancing the texture appearance of surface elements like skin pores and wrinkles and other delicate structures.

5. Enhanced Dyntopo (Dynamic Topology)

- **Faster Dyntopo**: The Dyntopo tool now achieves faster performance since its capability to speed up sculpting operations. The tool enables rapid operation speed with heavy mesh models and it delivers superior details transitions during user interactions.

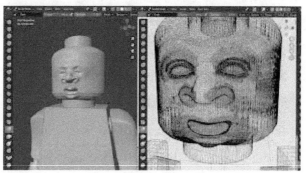

Dyntopo in Blender

- **Sculpt Detail Control**: Users can use simple controls on the Dyntopo interface to set detail precision for their sculpting work. Users can specify exact target detail thresholds with the tool through their current view or zoom position to enhance system operation speed.

6. Enhanced Cloth Simulation for Sculpting

- **Interactive Cloth Sculpting**: Users now have access to optimized cloth simulation capabilities through Interactive Cloth Sculpting after its integration into Blender 4.3 during the sculpting process. The system enables users to produce superior mesh details and produce realistic outcomes while providing total mesh control during operations.

- **Sculpting Cloth Deformation**: Users now have enhanced control to sculpt clothes and fabric objects and soft materials through better precision that enables them to generate authentic cloth deformations that match actual cloth responses to physical impact.

7. Sculpting Brushes with Physical Properties

- **Pressure-Sensitive Brushes**: The latest Blender version 4.3 enhances pressure sensitivity on tablets to allow users create delicate artwork through varying dimensions of tablet pressure. Different pressure levels are now detected by the brushes producing realistic organic strokes.

- **Tapered Brush Effects**: The new tapered brush effects provide artists with better precision when drawing lines to enhance their work on animal fur and hair elements along with organic shapes.

8. Improved Masking and Lasso Tools

- **Lasso Masking**: Blender enables artists to use its Lasso Masking features to obtain advanced selection and masking precision for intricate areas within their design projects. Sculpting operations through this tool will solely modify designated areas while maintaining the original state of everything else.
- **Advanced Masking Options**: The mask brush system received advanced capabilities that allow users to regulate intensity and fade levels for working precisely on selected areas without affecting other parts of their design.

9. Advanced Undo and History Tools

- **Better Undo System**: The Blender 4.3 update supports users with an enhanced undo algorithm which preserves faster performance throughout complex brushing operations. The improved action control system in Blender enables users to handle their undo-redo operations for added workflow security while protecting their essential modifications.

Undo System

- **Sculpt History**: The most current Blender release includes Sculpt History that allows users to observe their sculpt version development history through time traveling and permits them to restore previous states if needed.

10. Brush Presets and Sharing

- **Brush Preset Library**: The Blender 4.3 introduces Brush Preset Library as a brush storage system that makes it simpler for artists to handle their sculpting brush collections. The brush preset feature delivers frictionless management of artistic styling tools which artists must utilize in their art production.

- **Brush Sharing**: Brush sharing between users became better through direct export of custom brushes and community-brushed sharing methods to enhance artwork workflow when artists collaborate together.

The comprehensive sculpting capabilities of Blender 4.3 provide artists with enhanced control mechanisms and detailed sculpting performance in addition to workflow optimization and increases precision during software operation. All designers who handle complex poly meshes or subtle elements now experience improved workflows and tool enhancements during their different creative operations.

New Mesh Editing Features

Multiple new mesh editing tools included in Blender 4.3 deliver significant enhancements to model development work procedures. The mesh editing system in Blender has reached higher operational speed through an improved user interface and built-in strong features that deliver exceptional management capabilities for model shape and geometry. Mesh editing brings several crucial functions which represent the main aspects of Blender 4.3's release:

1. Enhanced Extrusion Tools

- **Extrude Along Curve**: The Extrude Along Curve utility provides users with tools to extend geometric shapes along curved lines to create intricate objects such as pipes alongside wires and individualized three-dimensional forms following exact dimensions.

- **Extrude to Face**: Users can perform extrusions directly to faces and edges through the Extrude to Face option as this tool simplifies mesh connection formation alongside existing geometry alignment.

- **Multiple Extrusion Modes**: The new Blender 4.3 version delivers several simultaneous extrusion capabilities that increase metal mesh fabrication production velocity. Through one operation users can execute multiple extrusion cycles to enhance their production rate.

2. Geometry Cleanup and Simplification Tools

- **Mesh Decimation**: The mesh decimation tool automatically reduces mesh polygon counts to preserve model shape with maintained details in the model. The optimization tool enables developers to enhance their models for applications in game development while using Virtual Reality and high efficiency visualizations.

Decimate Mesh

- **Mesh Cleanup**: The Blender version 4.3 includes automatic mesh cleaning tools that fix common modeling problems with degenerate faces alongside non-manifold edges and duplicate vertices. Smart features in Blender 4.3 improve the process of preparing meshes for export and cleaning imported meshes.

Mesh Clean up

- **Edge Collapse and Weld**: The edge collapse tool features a refined user interface to enable easy reduction of edges and vertices because of its better functionality. From within the new weld feature Blender joins vertices automatically while offering immediate execution of mesh topology enhancement.

3. Advanced Topology Tools

- **Quad and N-gon Topology Tools**: The 4.3 version of Blender presents fresh topology tools that help users build N-gons and quad-based complex shapes without facing topology problems. The tools allow users to keep mesh edge loop direction consistent through surfaces that use any topology beyond quadratic form.

- **Knife and Slice Tools**: In Blender 4.3 Knife and Slice Tools received improvements which boost the potential of cutting and slicing geometric objects. In Blender 4.3 users can perform uniform cutting of their geometry along axes while activating snapping tools and executing multiple slice operations using a single tool command.

- **Retopology Tools**: Inside the retopology system users gain new tools to make quick edge topology development possible while working on detailed models. The system delivers automatic mesh creation with surface alignment features which make retopology processes more efficient.

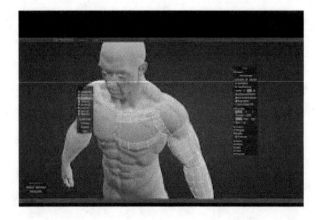

4. Snapping Enhancements

- **Face, Edge, and Vertex Snapping**: The enhanced systems of Face-Edge-Vertex Snapping provide users with more precise control capabilities during operations. Through the system users can execute exact snapping functions which connect between faces edges and vertices. Users can perform element connection between different mesh positions by snapping elements from point to line to face or face to face.

- **Magnetic Snapping**: The implementation of Magnetic Snapping lets vertices move towards one another using organic motion paths. Users obtain improved edge precision through precise control because edge movements occur through smooth continuous motions instead of interrupted snapping operations.

5. Mesh Mirroring Improvements

- **Symmetry Editing**: Symmetry Editing received improved modeling capabilities in Blender 4.3 because the software included new features for feature mirroring. Using Blender 4.3 users can perform complex geometry mirroring that operates across multiple axes and the capability to decide

33

which areas will be mirrored or excluded from the operation.

- **Live Mirror Updates**: The Live Mirror Updates system of Blender 4.3 shows instant mesh modification results to users without their need to change between different mirror modes.

6. Improved UV Unwrapping Tools

- **Automatic UV Unwrapping**: The most recent Blender version 4.3 delivers automatic UV unwrapping tools that produce UV maps for difficult meshes automatically while bypassing the need for user-led manual face unwrapping. The tool enables users to perform seam optimizations during which it also reduces texture distortion.

- **Pinning and Seam Adjustments**: The refined seam tools together with enhanced UV pinning features give users improved capabilities for two-dimensional mesh geometry unwrapping. The implemented adjustments lead to increased accuracy within texture mapping processes.

- **Live UV Editing**: Users can view mesh UV layout changes in real time through live editing within the editor during texture coordinate creation.

UV Unwrapping

7. Topology-Based Selection Tools

- **Edge Loop and Edge Ring Selection**: The software tools received upgraded selection features from Nucleus Design for Edge Loop and Edge Ring functions. Organic modeling tasks become more manageable because this update provides selection capabilities that enable users to pick particular segments of geometry.

- **Face and Vertex Group Selection**: The selection system now utilizes group organization to let users manage their geometry through a group-based system. The simplified model modification is possible through modifiers or animation processes because users can easily build and work with face and vertex groups.

- **Loop and Ring Grow/Shrink**: Loop and Ring Grow/Shrink gives precise control measures to help users perform better and more rapidly with edge loop and ring selections.

8. Mesh Deformation and Modification Tools

- **Deform Modifier Enhancements**: The developers added new features to the deform modifier that allow users to modify real-time mesh modifications efficiently. Users can use the subsurface scattering modifier through deformations to generate realistic organic forms because of enhanced modifier connections.

- **Lattice Modifier Integration**: The lattice modifier gained new features to give users a different way of performing mesh deformations. These mesh editing capabilities work better due to this feature which provides natural ways to modify mesh structures.

- **Topology-Aware Sculpting**: Users can experience topology-aware process transitions between modeling and sculpting when shifting modes with the help of new mesh tools. Proper topological consistency of geometry stays preserved during switching between all user modes.

9. Mesh Simplification and Optimization

- **Bézier Curve to Mesh**: The conversion from Bézier Curve to Mesh enables users to control mesh results as they perform operation steps. The tool lets users create complex paths before converting them into editable mesh shapes.

- **Optimized Edge Flow**: Blender 4.3 includes automatic edge flow optimization systems which let users enhance the topology of complicated models. Users obtain neat geometric shapes because this function enables automatic edge loop changes to generate deformation-ready animations.

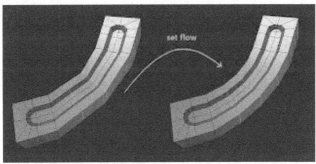

Edge Flow

10. Improved Modifier Stack Interactivity

- **Modifier Stack Workflow**: The modifier stack workflow received improved interactivity through modifications that enhance user-friendliness in

Blender 4.3. Users can interact with mesh geometry through modifier effects because they modify parameters on the mesh surface instead of accessing separate modifier panels.

- **New Modifiers**: The application includes two new modifiers: the bend modifier enables curved bending of meshes while the curve modifier allows users to deform meshes according to chosen axes.

11. Grease Pencil to Mesh Conversion

- **Grease Pencil to Mesh**: The Blender 4.3 release brought Grease Pencil to Mesh which allows users to convert their drawings into editible mesh geometry. The new update releases 2D-to-3D operation which converts sketches into editable 3D meshes that function properly for animation work and additional mesh editing.

Using Blender 4.3 users can achieve better efficiency through easy-to-use modeling tools that simplify complex procedures and boost both precision and tool flexibility. Users can now expedite organic as well as hard-surface modeling tasks using the upgraded mesh tools integrated into Blender 4.3.

Grease Pencil Improvements

In Blender 4.3 users have access to an extensive collection of Grease Pencil enhancements which enable them to design outstanding 2D and 3D animations and sketches together with illustrations within the Blender workspace. Blender 4.3 delivers enhanced workflow for Grease Pencil to fulfill advanced artistic drawing needs for traditional 2D artists and 3D Grease Pencil users. The main features of Grease Pencil improved in Blender 4.3 include:

1. New Stroke and Brush Features

- **Pressure Sensitivity and Dynamics**: The improved pressure sensitivity dynamics of Grease Pencil brushes allows artists to modify stroke width and flow and opacity at the same time by utilizing pen input pressure. New capabilities were added to brush dynamics through an upgrade which enabled jitter effects together with curvature and tapering features for brushstroke patterns.

- **Custom Brush Textures**: Artists now possess the ability to apply their custom brush textures to Grease Pencil brushes for creating unique stylized drawing lines according to drawing pressure and stroke speed controls. This opens up more options for organic, hand-drawn styles or custom ink effects.

- **Vector Brushes**: Grease Pencil now includes vector-based brushes as a feature that lets users create clean precise lines for creating artistic representations with aesthetic appeal.

2. Enhanced 3D Grease Pencil Integration

- **3D Drawing in Viewport**: The 3D Drawing in Viewport functionality in Blender version 4.3 provides users with the ability to make sketches inside three-dimensional drawing areas through Grease Pencil. Artists profit from a new interface that lets them build 3D drawings and annotate besides creating finished 3D environments while using control elements that merge 2D into 3D design approaches.

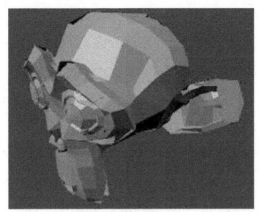

3D Viewport

- **3D Depth & Perspective**: The 3D drawing system now includes automatic drawing tools that adapt strokes to fit viewpoint depth and perspective to help artists draft proper 3D perspective-shape drawings quickly.

- **Object Layering**: The 3D Grease Pencil strokes can be broken down into individual object layers by users through Object Layering which optimizes the development of challenging 3D sketches and animated drawings. Stand-alone layers of two-dimensional drawings in three-dimensional environments allow artists to gain better control and visibility through positions.

3. Improved Animation Tools

- **New Timeline Features**: The timeline and Dope Sheet now encompass new functionalities that aid users in better controlling their Grease Pencil animation keyframes through improved management systems. Users now have superior keyframe regulatory capabilities that pair with the stroke-duplicating functionality due to enhanced interface timing controls.

- **Smoother In-betweening**: Blender 4.3 version introduces automatic smoother in-betweening functions to produce smooth transitions between keyframes in Grease Pencil animation. The system cuts down the need for human labor when performing frame-by-frame animation tasks.

- **Onion Skinning**: Onion Skinning received improved functionality through new upgrades that offer enhanced visibility during the preview of previous and following frames. Research indicates that viewing onion skins helps animators make smooth animations and detect animation progress through time. Users have precise control of onion skinning features to modify both its opacity and visibility properties.

Onion Skinning

4. Grease Pencil Sculpting Enhancements

- **Sculpt Mode Updates**: The Sculpt Mode received new features that enable enhanced Grease Pencil object sculpting by adding brush tools specialized for two-dimensional motion manipulation. Users obtain complete control to move their strokes manually and utilize the tool for expressive adjustments on the canvas.

- **Stroke Thickness Control**: Blender provides explicit controls for strokes thickness regulation through its sculpting toolset. The latest update delivers biomechanical techniques that let users modify stroke thickness without making any changes to geometry through editing or redrawing the base model.

- **Stroke Refinement**: The feature Stroke Refinement delivers enhanced drawing adaptability through its intended interface that helps users refine their pencil artworks.

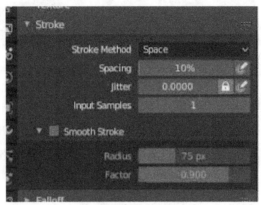

Stroke

5. Advanced Rigging and Deformation

- **Grease Pencil Rigging Improvements**: The new versions of Blender expanded rigging tools to help users work with Grease Pencil drawings. The latest Blender 4.3 release makes 2D character and scene rigging easier thanks to armature-based tools. Users create skeletons for their Grease Pencil objects faster to effortlessly modify object shapes.

- **Deform Modifier Updates**: The Grease Pencil deformation modifiers now let users make better changes to stroke deformations during animation tasks. Users can manage more effective and realistic shape transformations thanks to this upgrade.

- **Bone-Driven Shape Keys**: The introduction of Bone-Driven Shape Keys lets users link bone movement controls to shape keys for detailed deformations. The feature optimize the creation of 2D characters animations that need precise body and face poses.

6. New Material and Shader System

- **Advanced Materials**: The Blender 4.3 material system now supports Grease Pencil materials for creating high-quality appearance effects. Artists who use Grease Pencil in Blender 4.3 can easily add gradient fills and textured strokes plus advanced shaders to their drawing strokes to produce varied artistic outcomes.

- **Stroke-to-Fill Interaction**: The updated Blender 4.3 system improves how users apply gradient effects by connecting them to drawing strokes directly. Artists receive better control tools to reach their artistic goals both when filling solid areas and adding gradient patterns.

7. Simplified Workflow for 2D/3D Transitions

- **2D to 3D Conversion**: Blender 4.3 lets users convert 2D Grease Pencil drawings to 3D models more easily. The program provides smooth compatibility between 2D drawing and 3D modeling areas for creators to create between the two modes effectively.

- **View-based Drawing and Exporting**: Users can export Grease Pencil 3D strokes to different 2D locations using View-based Drawing and Exporting to mix 3D and 2D artwork in Blender. These artists benefit because their professional tasks become simpler across both media instructions.

8. Enhanced Export and Compatibility

- **Improved Export Options**: Blender 4.3 lets users export Grease Pencil data with better options that match Adobe Animate and Toon Boom software while giving improved quality for SVG and EPS outputs. The feature allows users to move their Grease Pencil content between animated software without losing original data quality.

- **Better Layer Management in Exports**: You now manage your export layers more effectively because the program lets you handle materials and layers when you transfer files to other file types. Users can preserve their separate layers with their specific settings when exporting to speed up transition between different programs.

9. New Grease Pencil Modifiers

- **Noise and Distortion Modifiers**: Blender 4.3 lets users add unwanted effects to Grease Pencil strokes by combining random or steady distortion methods. The new modifiers of Blender 4.3 lets artists produce strokes that look organic with a lively texture and enhance animations to appear more fluid.
- **Ripple and Wave Effects**: The Ripple and Wave Effect modifiers now help create smooth pattern movements on Grease Pencil lines to animate flowing hairs and leaking liquids better.

10. Interactive Interface Enhancements

- **Gesture-Based Drawing**: The new Grease Pencil interface enables tablet stylus users with modes that match the touch drawing experience for users. The system lets users adjust tools and make drawing strokes easily using menu controls and keyboard shortcuts so they do not need to stop creation.

- **Faster Workflow**: The new user design and keyboard shortcuts improve Grease Pencil object efficiency for artists. Drawing and sculpting switching in animation mode worked better with a new simple interface that made the process faster.

Blender 4.3 brings improved Grease Pencil functions that better combine 2D and 3D production pipelines for users. The platform enables users to bring their captivating work to life through both 2D drawing and full-scale rig development.

CHAPTER THREE

ANIMATION

Animation System Overhaul

Blender 4.3 brings faster animation processing paired with better interface features that let every animator create content more efficiently using advanced and practical tools. In Blender 4.3 the complete animation update applies to rigging and keyframing alongside character movement and video tracking plus non-linear video editing tools. These updates form the main changes that Blender 4.3 brought to its animation system:

1. Improved Keyframe Management

- **Keyframe Compression**: Keyframe Compression in Blender 4.3 improves data packing which protects motion accuracy while needing fewer keyframe entries. The new system increases animation processing strength particularly during extended sequences and advanced rig needs.

- **Easier Keyframe Navigation**: Blender 4.3 makes keyframe movement across both timeline areas simpler so users can locate and work with their keyframes swiftly. The system update with new keyboard commands helps users manage many keyframes more smoothly.

- **Multi-Keyframe Editing**: Users can edit all their keyframe animations collectively since Multi-Keyframe Editing works with the new mode to let them modify multiple movements at once. Multiple keyframes across the timeline become simpler to work with through this time optimization.

2. Advanced Graph Editor Improvements

- **Graph Editor Workflow Refinements**: Advanced updates to Blender 4.3 now makes both Graph Editor performance and interaction easier when you animate complicated scenes. Users get better ways to control splines and curves along with motion path tools through the latest system updates.

- **Keyframe F-Curve Adjustments**: The Graph Editor now provides precise F-Curve functions that help animators alter how the animation flow and movement behave plus its speed. Users can make their animations smoother by changing the keyframe tangents and curvatures directly.

- **Instant Preview**: You see active results of keyframe updates in real time without using the conventional timeline editing process. Using instant preview helps animators control their work better so they can see and improve their results quickly.

Graph Editor in Blender

3. Character Animation Enhancements

- **Pose Library and Pose Matching**: Pose Library and Pose Matching got new UI elements to make it easier to handle and store pose setups within the application. The new pose tools in Blender make character animations operate without interruptions during pose switching.

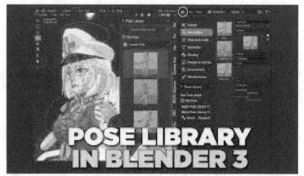
Pose Library in Blender 4

- **Auto-Rigging and Rigify Updates**: Blender advanced the auto-rigging and Rigify tools to speed up the construction of robust character rigs. Blender uses Rigify tools to adjust rig handling of complicated systems and create simple character rigs more easily.

- **Deformation Improvements**: Blender 4.3 includes enhanced tools that create natural deformed shapes when painting animation weights. The automatic weighting system works without operator involvement to enable testing and flexing of the rig system.

4. Non-Linear Animation (NLA) Enhancements

- **Non-Linear Animation Editor Updates**: The NLA editor updates in Blender 4.3 made it easier to mix and blend animations via a more efficient tool. With the NLA editor update Blender users see how their animations connect at once and build multiple action sequences including walks runs and static states without requiring individual fixes.

- **Action Strips and Transitions**: The product produces multiple new transition effects and makes it easier to create action strips which then blend animations automatically without the need for manual keyframe work.

- **Animation Layering**: In Blender 4.3 users can adjust how animation layers behave to bring out desired results. Animators can mix body and face movements together in separate layers plus they possess stronger layer switching functionality.

Animation Layering

5. Rigging and Control System Overhaul

- **Rigging Workflow Updates**: The software now offers many rigging updates that let users design detailed rigs fast and prepare them for animation work. The Auto-Rigging system develops its smart bone weighting technique to reduce manual effort and enhance rigging efficiency.

- **Constraint System Overhaul**: The 4.3 update of Blender includes a new constraints system that helps users efficiently join bones or objects into their rig with simple setup functions. Since the update our system became more flexible which helps users better control their parenting applications plus allows advanced IK settings and transformation adjustments.

- **Inverse Kinematics (IK) and Forward Kinematics (FK) Enhancements**: The software update brings new Kinematics features that let users build IK chains faster plus connect between inverse and forward motion with ease. Using both methods becomes essential to making natural characters move smoothly during animations.

6. Motion Capture and Tracking

- **Improved Motion Capture Integration**: The motion capture (MoCap) system within Blender 4.3 receives improvements by simplifying retargeting processes and handling external motion capture data more effectively. The new importing tools allow Blender users to refine data exactness leading to automatic fixes instead of manual additional work.

- **Improved Tracking Workflow**: It added upgraded features to handle cameras and objects in tracking operations. The system helps create a more realistic blend between filmed footage and 3D characters through their joint visual presentations.

Motion Capture and Tracking

7. Grease Pencil Animation Improvements

- **2D/3D Animation Integration**: The system now allows users to combine 2D Grease Pencil drawings and 3D scenery within Blender better than ever. With Blender users can create better hybrid animations because they can insert 2D characters into real 3D scenes.

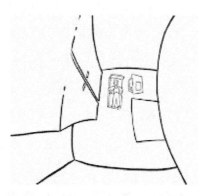

- **Stroke-Based Animation**: Animators can make top-quality 2D animations with the stroke-based tools in Grease Pencil while using Blender's full animation features to enhance their creations.

8. Animation Caching and Performance Improvements

- **Faster Playback**: Animation playback in Blender 4.3 has faster performance speeds that benefit all users working with complicated animation rigs and massive animation scenes. Animation scrubbing reaches higher performance levels because of the optimization techniques that reduce system delay.

- **Caching and Previews**: Efficient animation caching tools in Blender version 4.3 enable animators to preview animations through cache data instead of repeatedly playing the whole sequence. The program uses cache memory to save frames temporally in order to enable instant review of animations alongside improved system performance with intricate animation frames.

9. Real-Time Rendering and Preview Enhancements

- **Realtime Animation Previews**: The animation previews within Blender showcase real-time effects of materials and lighting as well as movement together with real-time rendering that avoids lengthy rendering delays.
- **Viewport Rendering Enhancements**: The viewport rendering features have undergone efficiency improvements that lead to improved duration speed when showing animated sequences. The rapid display of previews occurs during animation work because animators' scene changes and camera adjustments as well as their lighting

alterations show up immediately on their display screen.

10. Expanded Export Options

- **Improved Export for Animation**: Animation export capabilities have gained new options in Blender 4.3 that offer better compatibility between Blender users and other applications and game engines. The program provides users with improved rendering tools for USD, Alembic and Collada files in addition to its new FBX animation export features.

- **Character and Animation Export Enhancements**: Better connectivity between Blender 4.3 export features lets users transfer character rigs that contain weight maps as well as animation keyframes without major data corruption.

11. User Interface and Workflow Enhancements

- **Animation Tools Interface**: Through its animation tools interface Blender users gain easier access to user-friendly panels which help with character rigging and keyframing in combination with animation editing. The application provides new panels together with context menus that enable faster access to key animation operations.

- **Custom Animation Workspaces**: The Blender 4.3 release provides users with Custom Animation Workspaces which let them redesign their interface to suit various animation techniques such as character animation or motion graphics animation or camera animation.

Blender 4.3 used an updated animation system to develop innovative instruments and streamlined processes that enhance the speed of creating intricate animations together with improved user accessibility features. The combination of improved 3D character rigging technology and Grease Pencil 2D animation and motion capture data enhances all stages of an animation production workflow.

New Rigging Tools

Blender 4.3 features new rigging instruments which let users manage complex character rig structures and improve rig creation workflows and provide users with enhanced deformation manipulation tools for animation processes. Through new software updates riggers receive higher rig performance along with better interface functionality that enables freer rig structure design no matter what rigging tasks they need to complete. Blender 4.3 includes these major rigging improvements to its system according to the following list:

1. Auto-Rigging System Overhaul

- **Improved Auto-Rigging Workflow**: The Blender auto-rigging workflow in VERSION 4.3 features an entirely new system design that optimizes both speed and accuracy for setup creation. The new system code creates automatic bone placement while also providing assistance for skinning along with weight painting from chosen geometry. The system lets users conduct accelerated rigging operations for their characters.

- **Rigify Integration**: Rigify Addon received enhancements in the Blender automatic rigging system that resulted in superior outcomes. The updated version provides users with enhanced rigging setup capabilities together with adjustable rig elements and bone scale features for humanoid and quadruped characters.

- **Adaptive Rigging**: A rigging system detects difficult character characteristics through geometry analysis to produce better rigging structures optimized for nonstandard dimensional bodies.

2. New Bone Constraints and Controls

- **Bone Drivers**: The latest improvements to bone drivers now appear in Blender version 4.3. Using drivers in Blender allows users to make their bone positioning and rotational as well as scaling dependent on other objects or bones thus improving rig interactivity with both manual user input and external animation curves.

- **Custom Bone Constraints**: Blender 4.3 provides users with new bone constraints through its version release that brings advanced control over how bones integrate and connect with one another. The latest version of Blender 4.3 offers enhanced bone constraint functions by improving IK-FK blending capabilities and adding customized IK constraints with multiple control options to manage bone motility during rig making.

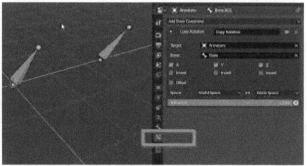

Bone Constraints

3. Inverse Kinematics (IK) and Forward Kinematics (FK) Enhancements

- **IK-FK Blending**: The IK-FK Blending feature in Blender 4.3 permits users to shift between FK and IK control methods on their unified rig through a spineless interface. Character animators gain from this feature which lets their rig perform IK for ground-foot planting before transitioning to FK dynamics for limb motions.

- **Better IK Setup**: The setup procedure for inverse kinematics chains simplified automatically after new implementation stages. The automatic IK positioner within the technology helps riggers enhance their working speed by dedicating less time to IK system set-ups for each character.

- **Improved IK Solvers**: The IK solvers in Blender 4.3 have received improved solutions that enhance natural motion accuracy through better solvers that address gimbal lock problems and offer additional stability when stretching bones during complex movements.

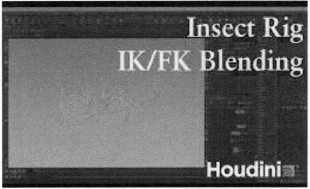

Inverse Kinematics and Forward Kinematics

4. Advanced Weight Painting Tools

- **Automatic Weight Painting**: The Blender 4.3 version offers new features for automatic weight painting that constructs bone weights through mesh geometry inputs. The weight painting features of Blender 4.3 automate rig system generation and produce advanced skinning solutions which save users from manual weight modification work.

- **Weight Painting with Proportional Editing**: The 4.3 software version of Blender added Proportional Editing functions which let users smoothly distribute weights during weight painting on selected mesh regions. Animation of mesh model bones produces fluid movement because this feature creates natural deformation effects on both thin sections and joint areas that must undergo gradual bending motions.

- **Relax and Smooth Weights**: Users in Blender 4.3 now have access to a refined weight relax together with smooth brush toolset which adjusts weight problems and creates symmetrical deformations throughout the entire rig system.

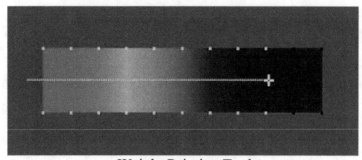

Weight Painting Tool

5. Pose Library and Pose Matching

- **Pose Library Enhancements**: Pose Library Enhancements in Blender 4.3 include major developments which furnish users with effortless poses saving capabilities and loading features. Users gained better pose matching capabilities through the update that enabled them to smoothly blend poses and execute their application on rigs with enhanced positional accuracy.

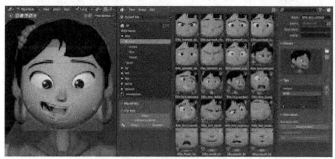

Pose Library

- **Pose Transitions**: In Blender 4.3 users can now create smooth move sequences between poses because the software adds automated intermediate pose generation along with pose combination tools.

6. Character Setup and Rigging Templates

- **Rigging Templates**: Built-in rigging templates serve character categories such as humanoid and quadruped creatures and vehicles under the Blender version 4.3 framework. The rig-making process becomes faster because Blender has pre-configured templates that combine automatic bone structures with foundation rigging and skin mapping functions.

- **Dynamic Rigging Adjustment**: Users benefit from dynamic rigging modification features in Blender 4.3 that enable them to make instant template adjustments while they work. Users can tailor the templates to fit specific needs since these templates maintain an entire rigging structure without modification.

7. New Rigging Operators and Tools

- **Rigging Operators**: The rigging operators in Blender 4.3 implement operational tools to help users accomplish fast rig component duplication and mirror and scaling operations. Among the operators in Blender 4.3 are command hotkeys and right-click menu context that help users speed up their rigging process for bone and control development and modification.

- **Bone Envelope Adjustments**: The rigging system now contains new control elements which simplify end-user modification of bone envelopes for regulating bone deformation areas. Riggers achieve better control of bone geometric influence through fine-tuning which enables them to produce natural deformed forms without weight painting requirements.

8. Control and Customization of Rig Controls

- **Custom Control Rigging**: Blender 4.3 version offers riggers the ability to build unique user interface controls through its improved custom control rig system that enhances animation workflow. The animation development process uses custom controls to enable users add facial sliders and pose state switchers as needed for their animation tasks.

- **Widget Customization**: The rigging system now features Widget Customization which provides users with novel ways to modify widgets that handle rigging elements based on visual tag components or handle elements to boost posing and manipulation functionalities. The system enables animations designers to create customized widgets for their rigs which boost animator comfort throughout the process.

9. Driver and Expression Support for Rigs

- **Custom Drivers for Rigging**: The rigging drivers incorporated into Blender 4.3 combine superior performance with highly usable features for end-users. Blender version 4.3 introduces a driver framework that enables users to make individual drivers for each bone while controlling which positions Pet programmers can use to outline complex relationships between rigging elements.

- **Expression Support**: The most recent Blender 4.3 update expands rig control abilities through its better expression capabilities. New mathematical expressions in drivers enabled animators and riggers to build sophisticated rigs that utilize various control parameters for their responses including bone rotation management of other controls and facial expression manipulation using sliders.

10. Rigging with Physics and Simulations

- **Physics-Based Rigging**: The physics simulation system of Blender 4.3 enables skeletal rigs to experience real-time responses to gravitational forces and wind effects and contact interactions. New programming functions for soft-body physics and cloth simulation became accessible to users through the application framework yielding authentic physics-based animation sequences.

- **Dynamic Rigs with Constraints**: The new constraint system permits bones to sense environmental forces when they encounter other simulation objects. The system now includes automatic external force reactions in characters and rigged objects to enhance user experience through decreased keyframing needs.

11. Performance Improvements for Rigging

- **Optimized Rigging Performance**: The latest version of Blender 4.3 presents superior performance improvements that enhance quick rigging work especially for intricate bone arrangements and significant deformation circumstances. The enhanced rigging operation speed among skinning and weight painting and posing functions allows quicker task completion resulting in reduced time-to-completion.

- **Rigging Cache**: The rigging cache system provides temporary data storage to enhance character and complex rig editing and posing times particularly for setups that employ many constraints and drivers.

12. Export Options for Rigs

- **Export to Game Engines**: The 4.3 version of Blender equipped users with advanced abilities to export their rigs towards gaming platforms including Unreal Engine and Unity. Users can migrate rigging setups with constraints together with skinning from Blender to external platforms because of improved bone and animation export features.

- **FBX and Alembic Enhancements**: FBX and Alembic export capabilities obtain improved features that improve complicated rig configuration and animated constraint and mesh deformation capabilities to preserve functional integrity when using external environments.

The rigging tools in Blender 4.3 let users design systems easier while controlling animation distortions through improved flexible approaches. Users now experience faster setup times along with easy pipelines to produce animated characters for games and simulations that produce genuine animations because of these rigging improvements.

Motion Capture Integration

Using Blender 4.3 users gain access to enhanced motion capture integration which makes it simpler to import and work with and use MoCap data for producing more realistic animations. Blender provides better usability by combining several file formats into one interface thereby simplifying workflow complexity between internal and external MoCap sources. The motion capture integration for Blender 4.3 introduces three main updates through which users can benefit:

1. Enhanced MoCap Data Import

- **Improved File Format Support**: Blender version 4.3 offers better MoCap file format handling by processing BVH, FBX and C3D, TRC and HUMANOID alongside its previous supported formats. Through the application users can effortlessly import their MoCap system data because it does not demand external plugins on popular devices such as Vicon, Xsens and Kinect.

- **Automatic Bone Mapping**: The automatic Bone Mapping system in Blender 4.3 automatically assigns bone matching during MoCap data import procedures using its new update. The automatic bone matching capability in this workflow automates the process of merging MoCap skeleton information correctly with your rig bones without the need for extensive manual interaction.

- **Import MoCap to Armatures**: You can use Import MoCap to Armatures to insert Motion Capture data directly into your Blender armatures thus enabling automatic keyframe adjustments between the MoCap motion and your armatures. The improved workflow procedure enables users to transform character animation with Motion Capture data without distorting the existing sequence instead of building a new animation from scratch.

2. Retargeting and Mapping Improvements

- **Retargeting MoCap Data to Different Rigs**: Blender 4.3 provides users with a retargeting system that allows MoCap data transfer from one skeleton to another regardless of their divergent rig structures. The system uses target-rig proportional measures and bone structures and positional constraints to adjust motion data which produces animations featuring natural movement dynamics.

- **Bone Adjustments for Different Proportions**: The software allows users to customize MoCap data selections before moving animation data from one character to another with unmatching height structures between humans and creatures as well as child and adult versions. Users can use these tools to perform easy bone adjustments and rotation modifications and scaling adjustments that produce accurate motion results on the new rig.

- **Simplified Retargeting Workflow**: The retargeting tools in Blender 4.3 have a streamlined workflow through automatic bone connection mapping that leads to quick rig deformation. You can operate retargeting more smoothly since complex menus and settings are not visible.

3. MoCap Data Cleanup and Editing Tools

- **MoCap Data Cleanup**: The unregulated quality of motion capture takes place in environments that yield MoCap data containing excessive noise together with multiple erroneous elements. The Blender 4.3 edition includes updated tools to handle standard data problems that generate unwanted animation movements or erratic motions detected in original animation data. The tools improve the quality of animation curves leading to improved capability for people to refine MoCap-based animations better.

MoCap Data Cleanup

- **Keyframe Editing**: Users can edit MoCap keyframes with improved tools located inside the Dope Sheet as well as the Graph Editor. Through the editor interface users receive immediate access to keyframe timing adjustment tools while having a tool that allows smoothing of motion curves to improve animation efficiency.

- **Noise Reduction and Smoothing**: The MoCap noise reduction filter in Blender 4.3 functions as an enhancement tool for MoCap data by means of smoothing techniques. The filter function in Blender 4.3 transforms unrefined MoCap data into smooth sophisticated motions that maintain natural appearance.

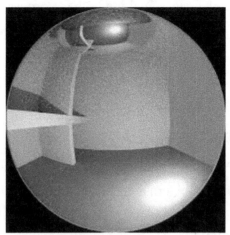

Reducing Noise

4. Facial MoCap Integration

- **Facial Motion Capture Support**: Blender 4.3 features complete support for Facial Motion Capture through its interface with FaceWare as well as Apple's ARKit. The system allows users to import MoCap facial data before applying it to facial bone-rigs to produce realistic character facial expressions as well as synchronized speech.

- **Automatic Lip Syncing**: Automatic lip-sync functionality based on facial Motion Capture data becomes possible with Blender 4.3 through the newly released tools. Your method of recording oral movements serves to connect with suitable phonemes which inserts them into your character's facial rig making the process ofAnimate synchronized speech and expressions simpler for creators.

5. Real-Time MoCap Capture

- **Live MoCap Capture**: In Blender 4.3 users gain access to real-time motion capture capturing through external tracking equipment that combines cameras with depth sensors as well as motion control suits including Xsens and Perception Neuron. Real-time MoCap streaming data connections with Blender enabled engineers to provide animators with the chance for instantaneous feedback.

- **Motion Tracking for Real-Time Capture**: Real-Time Motion Tracking within Blender 4.3 functions via tools that track objects and markers they find by using cameras and sensors with external devices. Through this system Blender generates motion-capture information about full bodies and individual objects thus expanding its animation capabilities.

6. MoCap Editing and Post-Processing Tools

- **MoCap Post-Processing**: MoCap Post-Processing tools of Blender 4.3 help users improve MoCap data after import and retargeting to help them optimize their motion results. Users can manage their animations through the tool which offers movement smoothing tools and speed control settings while providing functions to edit motion curves for fixing irregular joint motions and stretching.

- **Corrective Pose Tools**: Blender 4.3 brings forth corrective pose tools which enable direct animation key changes that address MoCap data deficiency problems. In situations where MoCap data presents limited precision animators can apply these tools for final animation to obtain the needed style.

- **Animation Layers**: Animation Layers via NLA (Non-Linear Animation) strips permits Blender 4.3 users to combine hand-keyed animations and MoCap data with other MoCap data sources into one seamless transition during multipurpose editing.

Animation Layers

7. Motion Capture and Game Engine Compatibility

- **MoCap Data Export for Game Engines**: The latest update in Blender 4.3 now enables better Motion Capture data export function for use in both Unreal Engine and Unity game engines. The export mechanism properly preserves both Motion Capture keyframes as well as retargeted and rigged data so they play back correctly in game engine applications.

- **Improved FBX Export**: The optimization of FBX export enhances data transfer performance by ensuring correct storage of imported MoCap rigs and animations during the export process. Developers who use interactive animation platforms cooperate with animators to maximize the benefits of this export process.

8. MoCap Data Visualization and Analysis

- **Visualization Tools**: The latest Blender version 4.3 includes visualization tools to assist animators during their inspection of MoCap data. During inspection both motion paths of bones and keyframe curves from MoCap can be displayed within the Graph Editor interface. The efficient operation of animation refinement and quick troubleshooting becomes achievable through this specific feature.

- **Motion Path Analysis**: Visual displays generated through motion path analysis help animators track temporal bone as well as object movements. The detection of abnormal limb positions and incorrect postures happens through professional animation use of this technology during their evaluative process.

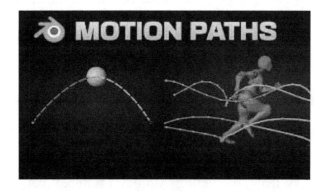

9. MoCap and Character Rigging Integration

- **Auto-Rigging for MoCap**: The Auto-Rigging system of motion capture in Blender 4.3 gets better processing capability for handling captured motion data. A rig for MoCap characters can rapidly create itself before automatically readjusting its position based on incoming motion data. This system stands out as the perfect solution for dealing with custom or non-standard rig characters that appear in your projects.

- **Rigging and MoCap Hybrid Workflows**: This new Blender 4.3 version presents a mixed workflow which unites custom rigs with Motion Capture data to allow users to orient MoCap data alongside manually animated elements. Users benefit from this capability since it helps them refine animations from faulty MoCap data but also enables them to generate additional animations and perform tricky movements.

10. MoCap Tools for Virtual Production

- **Virtual Production Integration**: The Blender 4.3 software now connects to virtual production systems by letting Motion Captured data match live-action video streaming. Software real-time integration with virtual set tracking enables virtual production teams to make realistic visualizations of actual environments.

- **MoCap in Real-Time Viewports**: Users obtain improved real-time MoCap data visibility in the 3D viewport of Blender 4.3 which permits them to inspect and adjust MoCap processes during virtual environment interaction.

11. MoCap Retargeting and Cleanup for Facial Animation

- **Facial MoCap Data Cleanup**: Blender 4.3 provides tools to cleanse Facial Motion Capture data that enhances expression accuracy through removal of data-altering components. As facial tracking devices work with cleaned data during the process it leads to increased import quality.
- **Facial Rig Retargeting**: Users can now straightly transfer Motion Capture facial expressions to their own individual facial rig constructs through Blender's Facet Rig Retargeting function for better character rig animation quality.

The Blender 4.3 software release integrates motion capture tools that improve data transfer across animation pipeline stages from import to retargeting functionalities and cleanup and export operations. The Blender 4.3 release provides users better tools to produce realistic time-efficient MoCap-based animations.

CHAPTER FIVE

RENDERING

Cycles and Eevee Updates

In its latest version 4.3 Blender software gives important enhancements to its two principal rendering engines Cycles and Eevee. The upgrades provide artists with superior results delivered faster through higher design possibilities and better quality performance standards. The Cycles rendering system and Eevee engine receive their main feature updates in Blender 4.3:

Cycles Updates

The general physical path-tracing engine Cycles present in Blender lets users experience precise lighting effects along with superior rendering performance.

1. Faster Rendering with Adaptive Sampling

- **Adaptive Sampling**: The latest update to Cycles in Blender 4.3 contains an improved adaptive sampling technology. Automatic scene analysis leads the system to adapt sample counts based on complexity levels so detailed regions get denser sampling but homogenous regions receive less samples. The combination between adaptive sampling technology and this update boosts the performance of rendering as well as improves visual quality when working with complex scenes that feature extensive detail variations.

Adaptive Sampling

- **Sample Clamping**: The sample clamping option in the new adaptive sampling system controls noise levels through maximum sample limitations for areas with minimal details.

2. AI Denoising Enhancements

- **AI Denoiser Improvements**: AI denoiser capabilities in Blender 4.3 demonstrate better progress because they reduce noise effectively while preserving detailed elements of the rendered image. Image accuracy increases with dust-free results because the final rendering system achieves enhanced performance in high-contrast areas and operations with reduced sample counts.

- **Real-Time Denoising**: Users receive instant feedback about denoised results when working with the AI denoiser because it operates efficiently during real-time rendering tasks. Better performance assessment methods help artists complete visual effects for their scenes.

3. More Accurate and Flexible Light Sampling

- **Improved Light Sampling**: The latest Blender version 4.3 improved Cycles light sampling capabilities for reducing noise during multiple light reflections while producing glare effects. New sampling capabilities improve the accurate reproduction of reflective materials therefore making redundant excessive sample use.

- **Better Light Paths for Complex Materials**: Blender version 4.3 improves its processing of complex materials like glass and water through enhanced light sampling techniques which generates clearer rendering output while reducing total rendering times.

4. GPU and Hardware Acceleration

- **GPU Rendering Improvements**: The implementation of GPU rendering enhancements enables Cycles to accelerate performance on GPU hardware devices when using AMD or NVIDIA hardware systems. Current GPU hardware technology enables new releases to achieve unprecedented speedups in the rendering process. The system provides users with capabilities to handle big projects followed by complex calculation requirements.

- **CUDA and OptiX Optimization**: The Blender 4.3 version improves the compatibility between CUDA and OptiX by integrating ray tracing capabilities from OptiX with CUDA framework developed by NVIDIA. NVIDIA RTX GPUs experience faster real-time ray tracing through these technologies thus achieving maximum speed from existing hardware.

5. Viewport Rendering Enhancements

- **Viewport Quality Improvements**: The Blender 4.3
  version boosted viewport rendering functions at
  various speed levels and output quality through
  improvements that let Cycles viewport operations
  work more smoothly with high-definition textures
  and complex lighting setups. Multiple renders no
  longer hold up users from scene adjustment since
  they can proceed without waiting for complete
  outputs.

6. Cryptomatte and AOVs (Arbitrary Output Variables) Enhancements

- **Cryptomatte Support**: Blender has improved its
  Cryptomatte tool in the Blender 4.3 version to make
  Cycles rendering more suitable for compositional

work. Blender users gain post-production automation through this enhancement to produce matte passes for complex materials and object layers so they can more easily manipulate post-productions elements.

- **AOVs Enhancements**: AOVs Enhancements in the software enhance control of Arbitrary Output Variables rendering passes which benefits users creating complex VFX and animation content.

7. Motion Blur Improvements

- **Improved Motion Blur**: Cycles in Blender 4.3 enhances motion blur functionality by applying advanced sampling technology to moving scene objects for achieving authentic realistic effects. Motion blur effects in the newest update create natural flow during fast-moving element renderings that include vehicles and moving active characters.

Motion Blur Improvements

Eevee Updates

Most users find real-time rendering engine Eevee stunning because it combines speedy computational abilities with stunning visual effects during interactive performance.

1. Improved Ray Tracing and Reflections

- **Ray Tracing for Reflections**: Using ray traced reflections allows Blender 4.3 users to achieve realistic reflection effects on glass and metal surfaces through the Eevee rendering mode. Real-time accurate reflection computations introduced through this update make it possible to eliminate the requirement for cube maps and screen-space reflection methods.

- **Refraction and Transparency Enhancements**: The Eevee program made its transparent materials more effective through better capabilities in dealing with refraction and transparency. The management tools for refractive elements in this update designed better monitoring techniques that simplify the creation of viable realistic results without compromising system performance.

2. Screen Space Global Illumination (SSGI)

- **SSGI Updates**: The Screen Space Global Illumination system within Blender 4.3 attained several updates which delivered both better performance statistics and enhanced indirect lighting precision for Eevee. Eevee performs lighting reflections modeling as it smoothes shadowed areas to improve the realistic appearance of complex lighted elements.

- **Better Light Interaction**: SSGI demonstrates better light interaction capabilities through advanced handling of glass water and metallic materials hence producing enhanced real-time lighting effects.

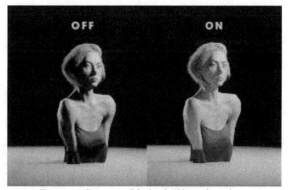

Screen Space Global Illumination

3. Improved Depth of Field (DoF)

- **Enhanced Depth of Field**: The upgraded DoF capabilities in Blender 4.3 combine better quality bokeh effects with enhanced operational smoothness through its Eevee engine. New adjustments in the DoF system by developers resulted in improved control of focal planes and aperture mechanisms resulting in superior visual results.

- **Lens Effects and Bokeh**: The Eevee engine in Blender 4.3 provides a new depth of field reproduction system with its Lens Effects and Bokeh features enabling users to achieve camera-like blur effects in their shallow depth of field photographic Recognitions.

Depth of Field (DoF)

4. Improved Ambient Occlusion (AO)

- **AO Updates**: The updated ambient occlusion (AO) functions of Eevee generate accurate shadows and improves the definition of hidden areas and solid angles. AO now functions at higher speeds as part of its updated version so users can have better real-time capabilities when creating 3D environments with complex features.

- **Volumetric Ambient Occlusion**: Volumetric Ambient Occlusion is included in the update because it provides shadow management and indirect illumination for volumetric elements consisting of foliage and smoke to provide atmospheric effects in real-world scenes.

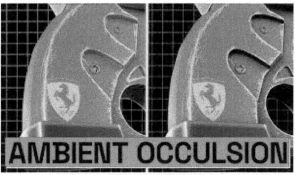

Ambient Occlusion (AO

5. Performance and Memory Optimizations

- **Better Performance on Complex Scenes**: The Blender 4.3 version includes Eevee performance improvements that optimize complex scene handling when users work with expansive geometric models and various lighting elements. Rendered scenes become more responsive and provide users with better real-time feedback opportunities through the optimized performance.

- **Memory Efficiency**: Eevee's memory optimization functions protect system stability by reducing crashes when handling big scenes thereby ensuring safety for users who want to extend their performance limits.

6. Volumetrics Enhancements

- **Volumetric Effects**: Eevee received better volumetric effects through its latest updates which deliver enhanced fog and smoke attributes alongside improved light scattering capabilities for volumes. The most recent update gives additional depth together with ambience which improves how see-through materials look in scenes.

- **Interactive Volumetrics**: Eevee introduces interactive volumetrics that accelerates volumetric rendering and increases the developer response time for creating intricate smoke and fog outcomes.

7. Light Probes and Reflections Probes

- **Reflections Probes**: Under the Reflections Probes feature Eevee obtains new parameters to work with reflecting probes. The probes enable exact reflection information delivery to elements inside a setting during work with reflective materials. Probes can now be established more quickly while users access sophisticated options to produce realistic real-time reflections in their projects.

Reflections Probes

- **Light Probes**: Under improved indirect lighting control in Eevee Light Probes generate authentic lighting effects for structures that show reflections and refract light.

8. Viewport Rendering Enhancements

- **Real-Time Quality Improvements**: The viewport renderer in Eevee underwent an upgrade to deliver enhanced quality view viewing functionality when working on scene content. Users must leverage this functionality because it enables real-time performance of complex material applications together with volumetric elements while using lighting features.

- **Improved Lighting Feedback**: Artist edits their scenes with real-time feedback in Eevee because the viewport shows output which corresponds to the actual final render.

General Improvements for Both Engines

- **Updated Materials and Shaders**: The material and shader capabilities of Cycles and Eevee function identically when users make use of upgraded nodes with better material handling to create equal visual results in real time and high-end rendering modes.

- **Better HDRI Support**: The latest release provides better HDRI accommodations which make high-quality HDRI image application simpler in environment mapping and lighting systems.

- **Improved UI for Render Settings**: Blender 4.3 introduces an advanced Render Settings user interface that let users move between Cycles and Eevee configurations through a streamlined parameters adjustment interface.

Blender 4.3 provides better rendering speed plus advanced rendering tools for Cycles and Eevee users. Artists get more work done with better creative choices that produce better render quality results across all their VFX and real-time projects.

New Render Settings

Blender 4.3 updated all parts of the Render Settings to give users new features while making controls easier to configure. Blender 4.3 workflow adjustments most favor artists who work with complex scenes and require personalized rendering settings for both Cycles and Eevee. Blender 4.3 Render Settings sees these main updates and editions in its inventory:

1. Unified Render Settings Interface

- **Simplified Layout**: The new Blender 4.3 interface now makes it easier to set render settings because of its more intuitive layout. Users find all their render settings easier to access because settings are grouped into five sections such as Output, Sampling, Lighting, Shading and Post-Processing.

- **Cycle vs. Eevee Toggle**: Users can choose between Eevee and Cycle rendering through a simple on-off switch in the Render Settings menu to make rendering decisions faster. The user interface automatically shows matched options when they switch between rendering engines.

2. New Sampling System

- **Adaptive Sampling**: Blender 4.3 uses an automatic system that changes the number of pixel samples according to scene details. The new adaptive sampling system changes sample quantity by itself to keep detailed areas sharp while saving resources on simpler parts. To make automatic noise reduction better you can change the Noise Threshold setting on adaptive sampling. After rendering stops when the noise meets or surpasses the set threshold level which reduces computations in less detailed areas to give better performance.

- **Noise Threshold for Adaptive Sampling**: The adaptive sampling tool has a Noise Threshold slider users may adjust to handle noise reduction levels. The system ends rendering when noise values hit specific minimum points to save rendering time on insignificant areas.

- **Denoising Options**: Through the Render Settings the user now selects between multiple denoising options and AI Denoiser works for both rendering engines Cycles and Eevee. Updated denoising techniques supply superior noise removal while saving delicate detail retention in targeted areas.

3. Improved Motion Blur Settings

- **Motion Blur Enhancements**: The Blender 4.3 system updates provide better motion blur management for both Cycles and Eevee through their advanced setting options. You can now control the motion blur impact more accurately on speedy motions plus camera movements.

- **Shutter Control**: Users can now set the exact shutter speed at any point through a single control slider that delivers precise motion blur effects to delayed shots.

- **Simplified Motion Blur Setup**: Users now have a simplified method to set Motion Blur through the Render Settings online interface for all engines and materials.

Motion Blur

4. Render Resolution and Output Settings

- **Custom Aspect Ratio**: Users in Blender 4.3 can select custom aspect ratios when rendering which makes them export various screen sizes suitable for different projects such as film production or social media purposes.

- **Render Scaling and Output**: The new tool enables users to change render sizes at the output stage of their projects. You can make rendering faster by changing scale settings which let you maintain aspect ratio locking or set unique output dimensions.

5. Faster GPU and CPU Switching

- **GPU/CPU Render Switching**: Our system now makes it faster for users to switch between CPU and GPU rendering choices which work in both Cycles and Eevee. Blender 4.3 makes smart decisions about rendering hardware selection to pick the most effective device.

- **CUDA and OptiX Support**: The NVIDIA GPU rendering software CUDA and OptiX has received performance enhancements that improve stability while utilizing supported graphics processing technologies.

6. Post-Processing and Compositing Updates

- **Built-in Post-Processing Effects**: Blender 4.3 offers Direct Post-Processing Effects inside Render Settings which helps users combine glow effects with chromatic aberration and lens distortion without needing the Compositor. Built-in settings let users make instant image style upgrades when they render results.

- **Layered Post-Processing**: Users can now modify different effects on multiple render passes or objects with Layered Post-Processing features which gives better control over the final outcome.

7. Render Passes and AOVs (Arbitrary Output Variables)

- **Improved Render Passes**: Blender 4.3 lets users work with better managed render passes through AOVs by enhancing their AOV system controls. Users in Render Settings now create and operate their preferred custom render passes with available elements such as diffuse, specular, shadow and reflection.

- **Multi-Layered AOV Output**: AOV technology offers advanced rendering technology that allows artists to make layered file output suitable for compositing. The rendering tool lets users adjust render passes independently for advanced processing without needing extra rendering passes.

8. Real-Time Viewport Rendering

- **Viewport Quality Settings**: Blender 4.3 now allows users to manage detailed quality parameters while their viewport renders. When users need to work they can view high-quality previews in their scene view and they can choose sample rate settings together with resolution and denoising controls to optimize viewport speed.

- **Viewport Ray Tracing**: Take renders real-shadow reflections and reflections that match final results without needing actual render time. The enhanced feature improves reaction time since it supports users who work with polished materials and complex lighting designs from several sources.

9. Ray Tracing and Realistic Shading

- **Realistic Material Shading**: The master component of render settings lets Eevee and Cycles users edit subsurface scattering settings and adjust metalness and roughness immediately.

- **Ray Tracing for Eevee**: Blender 4.3 now enables Eevee ray tracing to instantly render reflections, refractions and glass-like textures in its responsive mode The real-time rendering of Eevee enhances realism when the engine deals with reflective surface elements such as glass or water.

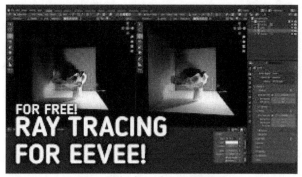
Ray Tracing for EEVEE

10. Output File Formats

- **Expanded Output Format Options**: Blender 4.3 offers users better management of rendering quality by adding support for OpenEXR as well as TIFF and WebP image formats and the FFmpeg animation export format.
- **Single and Multi-Frame Render Support**: The Blender 4.3 release offers advanced users better options for exporting work to OpenEXR alongside

TIFF and WebP for image files and FFmpeg for animated content.

11. Batch Rendering and Network Rendering

- **Batch Rendering Improvements**: The batch rendering capabilities in Blender 4.3 have evolved to make parallel scene or frame rendering easier to use. The user interface now helps people manage multiple render tasks effortlessly.

- **Network Rendering Support**: The system simplifies network rendering duties so you can distribute work to different computers in a render farm setup and scale up big projects.

12. Environment and Lighting Settings

- **Light Probes and Reflection Probes**: Users can better control lighting in complex scenes through Eevee real-time render engines since they can set more light probes and reflection probes effectively. An enhancement of the lighting system leads to better reflection details and produces natural indirect illumination.

- **HDRI Lighting Updates**: Thanks to latest HDRI Lighting updates the 3D software now uses HDRI images to bring better lighting results to scene environments.

13. Render Preview Improvements

- **Real-Time Render Previews**: Striking visual feedback becomes available faster because Blender 4.3 offers better preview functionalities of both Cycles and Eevee rendering systems. Viewers enable artists to modify scene properties instantly on real-time previews without switching screens.

- **Interactive Lighting and Material Feedback**: The system shows updated materials and lighting details with textures right after users change settings which speeds up their work especially for surface adjustments.

14. New Render Queue System

- **Render Queue Management**: The latest Render Queue tool helps users control their rendering tasks better. By using the render queue interface artists can get multiple scenes or shots ready for automatic processing then watch the output steps sequence automatically without human intervention.

With new Render Settings Blender 4.3 enhances performance while making operations faster and easier to control final results. The platform updates within Cycles path tracing and Eevee real-time rendering let users build easier methods to control their finished outputs.

Performance Optimizations

Placing Blender 4.3 into action creates more efficient work tools while making render times shorter and limiting how much system resources the application uses. The program changes make both immediate screen presentations faster while improving rendering lengths and system performance. The significant new capabilities in Blender 4.3 consist of these filters:

1. GPU and CPU Optimization for Cycles

- **Faster GPU Rendering**: After upgrading to Blender 4.3 users enjoy faster graphics card speed acceleration especially for their NVIDIA and AMD devices. The new system takes advantage of current GPUs benefits through CUDA and OptiX support on RTX cards to make rendering fast for scenes with many details.

- **Improved GPU Memory Management**: The advanced GPU memory management system enables users to use more complex scenes because it smartly allocates and distributes GPU memory so that memory limits and crashes do not occur.

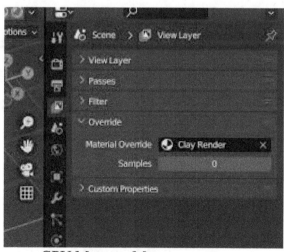

GPU Memory Management

- **Cross-Vendor GPU Support**: Under 4.3 Blender supports OpenCL and Vulkan for better GPU relationships between different brands. The improvements to AMD GPU system performance made both equipment types more stable and faster over different hardware environments.

2. Multi-Core CPU Rendering

- **Optimized Multi-Core CPU Utilization**: The new Blender 4.3 update designs CPU core utilization to help users efficiently use their multiple processors for rendering operations. The new distribution method for rendering lets users use their multi-core CPUs better to get fast results in less time.
- **Threading Improvements**: The update improves thread usage for scene preparation simulations and rendering by unlocking more CPU threads. This enhancement makes performance better during simulations that require complex resource usage.

3. Adaptive Sampling in Cycles

- **Faster Convergence with Adaptive Sampling**: You will now reach the desired result earlier with adaptive sampling on Blender 4.3. When adaptive sampling detects basic elements and smooth light effects in the scene it decreases the sampling resources used to prevent useless calculations.

- **Noise Threshold Control**: Through noise threshold settings the render process can automatically pause operations when target noise levels become acceptable thus consumed rendering time is optimized.

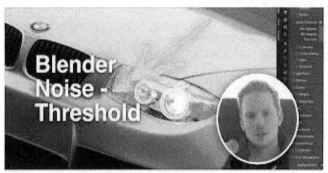

Blender Noise Threshold

4. Viewport Performance Improvements

- **Viewport Interactivity Boost**: The updated viewport system in Blender 4.3 makes live view better when you combine high-texture quality with detailed geometry. Users achieve better scene navigation because this speed update makes their interactions with lights materials and shaders happen faster.

- **Optimized Viewport Shading**: The viewport shading tool Eevee computer software makes it possible to display final-quality previews in real time without interrupting basic frame rate performance. The performance improvements in selecting objects at the viewport help users do scene refinements faster.

- **Simplified Scene Drawing**: Blender 4.3 enhances the speed at which it renders entire scenes and their graphical elements. Both updates make editing a large object scene more smooth and prevent freezes from affecting your workflow.

5. Grease Pencil and 2D Animation Speedup

- **Faster Grease Pencil Performance**: Blender 4.3 puts less strain on Grease Pencil systems which helps users draw animations faster. Drawing remains smooth even with many Grease Pencil strokes and editing actions while the entire system supports faster 2D animation operations.

Grease Pencil in Blender

- **Improved 2D Rigging and Animation**: After optimization both 2D character rigging and animation run better using Grease Pencil tool.

6. Simulation Performance Enhancements

- **Faster Fluid and Smoke Simulations**: The new update 4.3 makes Blender perform fluid and smoke simulations more effectively. With enhanced fluid processing techniques the system runs better and needs less computing power whereas both smoke and fire simulations handle input and render updates quickly thanks to optimized memory handling.

Smoke Simulations

- **Rigid Body and Cloth Simulation Improvements**: Rigid object and cloth simulation systems now run faster and more reliably to process difficult cloth-textured objects faster.

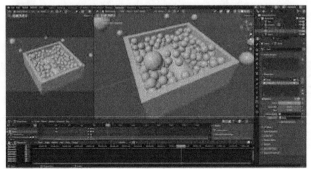
Cloth Simulation

7. File I/O and Asset Management

- **Faster File Import/Export**: Blender 4.3 improves how fast users can import and export data from all supported file types including FBX OBJ USD and Alembic files. The improved system lets users work faster when transferring their assets back and forth between Blender and other software programs.

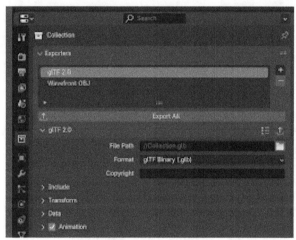

Faster File Import/Export

- **Improved Asset Library Loading**: The Asset Browser system handles asset library loading faster without any performance decrease from collection size expansion. The platform helps users who deal with sizable materials and animation assets by speeding up system access and enabling scene environment drag-and-drop features.

8. Memory Usage and Stability Enhancements

- **Reduced Memory Footprint**: The program takes up less memory space because updates lowered how data is stored and processed. Excessive scenes and texture-heavy problems require less memory use for best performance.

- **Stable Large Scene Handling**: When you work with big and complicated scene setups the new system handles memory better and saves information smarter to stop crashes and smooth processing on large models.

- **Thread Pooling for Background Tasks**: The thread pooling system manages background tasks such as caching and baking processes while handling simulation workloads in a way that prevents main workflow interference.

9. Eevee and Real-Time Rendering Optimization

- **Enhanced Eevee Ray Tracing**: Ray-traced reflections and shadows become faster when processing complex reflective or refractive objects in Eevee Ray Tracing performance improvements.

- **Improved Light Probes and Reflection Probes**: The system now updates betweener-probes and reflection-probes faster to add quick light controls and cut reflection time in large scenes.
- **Volumetric Rendering Optimization**: Users achieve better Eevee performance when they apply fog and haze effects to their scenes because Volumetric Rendering got optimized for lesser visual glitches.

10. Network Rendering and Render Farm Optimizations

- **Smarter Render Queue**: The smart render queue system now sends frame jobs to various machines or multiple processing queues to create renders faster and prevent idle times.
- **Better Render Farm Integration**: The network rendering setup works more efficiently because it sends tasks from a single machine to the connected computers. Users and studios who use render farms require this upgrade to produce animations or full scenes promptly and with high visual quality.

Render Farm

11. Viewport and Scene Data Management

- **Optimized Scene Data Handling**: Processing scene data becomes more efficient which gives usable assets faster while managing objects and assets operates at top speed. The system helps Blender run data handling jobs faster for users with complex setups which decreases their total waiting period.

- **Faster Object Instancing**: The latest Blender 4.3 version speeds up object re-use by optimizing the new object instance function. The optimization system frees up memory space in your system as it enhances the performance of projects which heavily use instances particularly when building forests or crowds.

12. File Loading Speed for Large Scenes

- **Efficient Scene Loading**: The new software version makes scene loading faster when dealing with large .blend files that hold many assets plus textures and simulation data. The system keeps better data organized and saves recent scene layouts to make project loading and work performance faster.

The new Blender 4.3 version enhances overall performance speed and allows easier control with all your simulation and animation tasks including rendering and artwork design. System upgrades create faster and improved processes to help users complete their assignments more quickly and with better results when facing demanding tasks or large projects.

CHAPTER SIX

SIMULATION

Fluid and Smoke Simulations Enhancements

New Blender 4.3 upgrades both performance and quality when simulating fluids and smoke. Security updates let users produce accurate simulations faster with improved performance that makes simulations run quicker. The upgraded water and fire simulation tools now let users create their effects more effortlessly. Blender 4.3 introduces major improvements that revolve around two essential aspects of fluid simulation:

1. Faster Fluid Simulations

- **Optimized Fluid Solver**: The fluid solver system now performs faster during complex fluid movement simulations. The new optimizations cut simulation runtime without changing the quality of results.

- **Improved Mesh Generation**: The new way to convert fluid simulations creates better mesh surfaces with fewer surface defects and smoother results. Flows through simulation show natural behavior while creating mesh results free from both simulation and surface distortion.

118

- **Adaptive Simulation Resolution**: The latest edition of Blender 4.3 features an advanced system that changes the fluid simulation resolution based on the scene conditions. The automatic scene view detection eases resource usage because fluid simulation resolution adjusts itself based on the scene layout. The tool creates a higher level of detail where moving liquid areas are active to enhance normal operation time in inactive regions.

Fluid Simulations

2. Real-Time Simulation Feedback

- **Improved Interactive Feedback**: The new system offers users enhanced response feedback while working with fluid settings and updating simulations simultaneously. The simulation process works better because you can instantly see how changes to the fluid area and objects impact simulation development and efficiency.

- **Simulating with Multiple Domains**: Blender 4.3 offers project areas that let users place many fluid domains together in one scene. The simulation system grows more flexible thanks to this feature because it lets users handle multiple liquid scenarios or combine different fluid types like water and oil together in one environment. When multiple fluid domains exist together they produce better results by decreasing error when they combine forces.

3. Enhanced Smoke and Fire Simulations

- **Faster Smoke Simulation Performance**: The current Blender release gives better performance results for smoke simulation work. The new smoke solver update makes simulation for time-sensitive smoke and fire scenes run faster. The system optimization makes smoke-fire interactions work better and saves visual quality while needing less computer power.

- **Improved Smoke Density and Detail**: System updates have resulted in better numerical control of smoke density and detail. The smoke solver modifications enable better realistic smoke-light interactions during object contact which enhances the visual experience. Improved small-scale smoke pattern management such as vortices and turbulence becomes accessible with higher resolution detail.

- **Better Fire Simulation**: Fire Simulation system grants users better control of flames because of its latest functional updates. Developments in smoke-fire interaction have enabled developers to produce genuine fire modeling simulations with spreading components and burning characteristics. The newly developed systems reveal larger fire explosion patterns in their simulations..

4. Volumetric Improvements for Smoke and Fluid Effects

- **Improved Volumetrics**: Through Blender 4.3 users gain better control of volume computation which applies to smoke and fire effects as well as fluid animations. The lighting behavior inside volumes improves significantly because the system now delivers precise light scattering and absorption thus enhancing smoke and fire effects. Advanced features in the software system make it simple for users to create stunning plumes plus glowing embers effects.

Improved Volumetrics

- **Faster Volumetric Rendering**: The rendering speed of volumetric effects namely smoke and fire effects now performs faster thanks to recent performance enhancements. The user achieves enhanced interactivity throughout scenes when they perform work because viewport speed and render completion time have improved.

- **Dynamic Volumetric Resolution**: With 4.3 Blender introduced an update which gives users real-time control to modify smoke and fire details and densities simultaneously. Higher system performance results from this setup because it improves resolution availability exclusively toward active smoke and flames while maintaining baseline resolution in background regions.

5. New Fluid and Smoke Interaction Features

- **Better Fluid-Solid Interaction**: More advanced fluid-to-solid interaction works better during operation. The new Blender 4.3 update fixes the collision behavior and fluid reactions when objects interact with static or moving elements during interactive scene view. The simulated fluid behaves more realistically by responding to objects and surface conditions.

- **Smoke and Fluid Interactions**: Under Blend 4.3 users can handle smoke and fluid interaction better to make steam and condensation simulations easier. Hot liquid passing into cold air generates natural steam flow from the surface. With simultaneous fluid behavior interactions these features produce more natural boiling and underwater volcanic eruption scenes.

6. Optimized Fluid and Smoke Caching

- **Efficient Caching System**: The refined caching system now makes fluid and smoke simulation run faster so baking and playback speed up. The new data caching system helps both reduce storage needs and speed up every simulation.

- **Support for High-Resolution Caches**: Blender 4.3 enhances support for storing fluid and smoke caches at high resolutions that keeps demanding simulations from slowing down system performance. The updates maintain proper performance and stability throughout simulation tasks with their heavy graphical content.

7. Smoke Density and Temperature Control

- **Advanced Smoke Temperature Control**: The current software update 4.3 adds complete temperature and density customization options to smoke production. Developers added new controls that help you adjust how smoke looks during temperature or density simulations which matter the most in creating practical fire effects or industrial smoke.

- **Realistic Buoyancy Effects**: Blender 4.3 adds proper smoke buoyancy effects that make particles behave realistically based on scene temperature values. Smokes react naturally when you apply temperature gradient or wind settings.

8. New Smoke Simulation Tools

- **Wind and Vortex Control**: The Blender 4.3 edition includes new elements for smoke simulation through wind and vortex force controls. These control features enable users to handle smoke movements accurately so winds and fire effects can produce the same impact without vortexes involved.

- **Turbulence and Flow Effects**: The new tools generate erratic smoke movements that bring realism to explosions and enhance their smoke clouds plus add credibility to tiny effects like blowing window air.

New Smoke Simulation Tools

9. Particle Interactions with Fluid and Smoke

- **Fluid Simulation as a Particle Emitter**: The current fluid simulation updates permit users to act as particle emitters for better handling of particles

125

based on how fluids flow. The tool makes effective displays when it displays fluid movement like water spray or foam movements.

- **Improved Fluid-Particle Interaction**: Blender 4.3 offers better performance for connecting fluid and particles together. Fluid motion that directs particle movement results in dynamic water impact effects including drop splashes and droplet spread. Particles feel the impact of effects coming from smoke and fire elements during their connected operations.

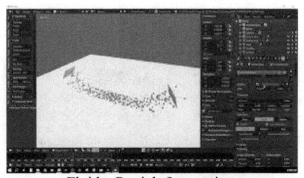
Fluid – Particle Interaction

10. Multi-Domain Fluid and Smoke Simulations

- **Multi-Domain Support**: With Blender 4.3 users can work with many fluid and smoke domains from one scene. This feature makes complex simulations run better by letting separate smoke and fluid areas react to each other naturally.

- **Cross-Domain Interaction**: Users can now connect smoke and fire simulations with liquids like water and lava through a single fluid system in Cross-Domain Interaction.

Summary of Fluid and Smoke Simulation Enhancements in Blender 4.3:

- Faster simulation performance and more efficient solvers.
- Real-time feedback for fluid, smoke, and fire simulations.
- Voluntary elements enhance precision when light scatters and is absorbed.
- The software connects smoke and fluid objects better to solid shapes while tightening the link between fire elements and fluid fires.
- The update includes both a new way to keep simulation data fresh and new equipment for better storage of this information.
- More detailed control over smoke density, temperature, and buoyancy.

- Different fluid-salt pairing scenarios work within our control system and liquid movement connections are better defined.
- Particle-driven effects and better integration with fluid systems.

Blender 4.3 tools now produce realistic smoke and fluid results faster which eases VFX creation across movie video game and other industries for their artists.

Cloth and Hair Simulation Updates

Blender 4.3 now makes cloth and hair simulation handle better performance and allows artists to refine these features better. The latest system version lets artists make better art with simpler tasks by showing them how to use real cloth and fabric with real hair and fur in their work. The next sections detail all changes made to the program:

1. Improved Cloth Simulation Performance

- **Faster Cloth Solver**: The cloth solver now uses optimization tools to solve problems faster making high-level cloth effects more responsive. The new solver technology makes simulation quicker whether you use high resolution models or handle large scenes.

- **Better Collision Detection**: The cloth items in your scene collide better with all objects now that soft and hard materials appear together. The system improves its speed by stopping cloth parts directly from entering or passing through objects during fast object movements.

- **Simulating Complex Fabrics**: Using Blender 4.3 producing high-quality cloth simulations for difficult fabric types such as silk leather and denim became possible in a realistic style. The cloth solver handles different cloth types better and delivers better natural cloth actions and reactions.

2. Enhanced Cloth Dynamics and Behavior

- **Advanced Wind and Gravity Controls**: The simulation system developed advanced wind effects and gravitational force management with new controls. Our ability to better handle clothing reactions to changing environmental forces creates better dynamic scene results.

- **Pressure and Tension Control**: The Blender 4.3 version now offers better simulation options for pressure and tension which makes material handling easier for balloons and tent fabrics as well as force-stressed cloth items. With Blender 4.3 artists developed the power to set how cloth fiber tension responds to internal pressures.

- **Cloth Stretch and Compression**: Users now edit cloth stretching and compression better with the updated parameter options. Materials need adjustment during load situations and while modeling fitted clothing or fabric because actual stretching and compression need representation in this simulation environment.

3. Cloth Simulation Caching Enhancements

- **Faster Cloth Caching**: The new cloth caching method builds cache files faster especially when users work on large scenes. Users get faster simulation results while working because their computer performs cloth calculations faster.

- **Multi-Resolution Caching**: As part of its latest update Blender 4.3 provides multi-resolution caching so users can do cloth simulations at multiple resolution settings. You produce finer quality results in chosen simulation areas but keep basic cloth material fast.

4. Hair and Fur Simulation Enhancements

- **Faster Hair Simulation Performance**: This new version of Blender makes hair simulation work faster and delivers better results for both hair and fur features. Blender 4.3 uses new techniques to manage big hair particle loads which makes simulation faster despite high hair densities.

- **Hair Strand Physics Updates**: The updated hair physics now makes hair react more realistically to wind movements plus gravity-assisted actions. Updates let hair behave naturally by moving with the body and responding to force and generate electricity like effects.

- **Collisions Between Hair and Objects**: The new system permits hair strands to have reliable physical contact with items like actors and their garments. Our enhanced hair simulation solution lets separate hair strands touch and move against each other without destroying the visual quality.

5. Improved Hair Styling Tools

- **Enhanced Hair Grooming Tools**: Blender 4.3 gives users better options for working with their hair tools by adding new features to version 4.3. Advanced designing tools respond and move every hair strand in our hands allowing perfect control over hairstyles.

- **Strand-based Grooming**: Updated hair grooming works better when you apply it to single hair strands. The power to control single hairs delivers better appearance results and enables users to produce real-looking intricate hairstyles.

- **Control Over Hair Curvature and Bending**: Users now adjust both hair bend direction and contour changes better than ever. The updated software lets users generate authentic hairstyles that produce wavy results plus realistic fur effects when exposed to wind.

6. More Realistic Hair Shading and Rendering

- **Improved Hair Shading Model**: Blender 4.3 brings a new hair shading system that helps create accurate hair material results. Users gain better control over light effects because Blender 4.3 shows light accurately where it contacts hair materials. The modified rendering produces superior control over material transparency and enables variations of glossiness and coloring for hair or fur

- **Better Hair Lighting and Shadows**: Hair reacts correctly with scene lighting because shadows and reflections appear real within the strands. Through its shading model the software correctly permits light to pass through hair strands resulting in realistic hair or fur surface textures which work for both Cycles and Eevee environments.

- **Volumetric Hair Rendering**: This release of Blender 4.3 enables users to make materials for realistic fur brush that handle light scattering effectively. Thicker hair shows best light behavior because the system renders fur and hair accurately.

7. Multi-Physics Support for Cloth and Hair

- **Cloth and Hair Physics Interaction**: The Blender 4.3 edition lets users enhance cloth physics and hair collision performance in simulations. The two systems advanced their collaboration during simulations that show characters whose hair and cloth must interact naturally like how clothes get entangled in hair.

- **Improved Cloth and Hair Pinning**: The add-on update provides enhanced techniques for joining cloth to hair pins that enable users to link precise cloth and hair locations with characters and items. The enhanced cloth and hair pinning system in updated virtual simulations helps users place

133

particular clothing and hair sections where desired including shirt collars and characters.

8. Wind and Force Field Effects for Cloth and Hair

- **Advanced Wind Forces**: New wind force rules trigger improved cloth material and hair interactions with wind patterns through better turbulence features and better gust management. New systems permit users to target specific cloth and hair regions when adjusting wind power parameters to produce subtle changes in wind simulation effects.

- **Localized Force Fields**: The new force field system lets users placed focused force zones on hair and fabrics for specific control. Users who know programming can modify force impact areas to produce better simulation outcomes.

9. Cloth and Hair Collision with Meshes

- **Better Mesh-to-Cloth and Hair Collisions**: The latest Blender 4.3 makes mesh-to-cloth and hair collision detection perform better. The enhanced mesh interaction makes sure the simulation works properly with complex cloth shapes and allows exact control over cloth material contacts.

- **Cloth and Hair Interaction with Rigid Bodies**: Through Blender 4.3 users can set precise cloth and hair collisions that prevent material penetration against solid surfaces and automatically move hair when body objects move.

10. Improved Hair Particle Editing

- **Hair Particle System Updates**: The latest Blender 4.3 release lets users manage their hair particle system better than ever. The tool update lets users handle their hair particles better while streamlining all hair styling actions.
- **Randomness and Variability**: The latest control system update for randomization and variety allows users to make better adjustments to their hair particle systems. Artists edit hair like real hair better with greater control when they change strand placements and dimensions including their hues.

Summary of Cloth and Hair Simulation Updates in Blender 4.3:

- Faster and more efficient cloth and hair solvers for better simulation performance.
- The new wind force controller helps objects move naturally alongside other effects.

- The system better detects when cloth and hair touch visible objects in the simulated environment.
- Blender 4.3 users benefit from advanced hair and cloth grooming tools that help control how the material looks and behaves interactively.
- The software updates its volume effects to match realistic hair and cloth rendering technologies.
- Better interaction between cloth and hair systems and other physics, such as rigid bodies and force fields.
- Speeding up caching and baking functions reduces the needed simulation time in both interactive and playback modes.

The Blender 4.3 changes let artists produce realistic cloth and hair simulations more effectively by reducing the technical difficulties of controlling dynamic special effects. The new capabilities give creators better options to design cloth and fur animations plus return results from soft bodies.

Physics and Rigid Body Updates

The latest Blender update integrates several important features that streamline physics operations including enhanced real-world rigid body handling. The updated system lets users control multiple physics processes faster when they simulate object collisions and fractures and manage constraints. These following improvements explain how physics and rigid body functionality works in Blender 4.3 version:

1. Faster Rigid Body Simulation

- **Optimized Rigid Body Solver**: The refined rigid body solver delivers faster and more dependable results during simulations that work with numerous objects. Simulation processing speed improvements help decrease workload and let users view results in real-time.

- **Improved Object Collisions**: The new collision algorithms of Rigid Body Collision Management make Blender 4.3 objects collide more accurately and lessen abnormal shaking during collisions. Collision simulation in the program provides better results and reliable outcomes due to its improved operation.

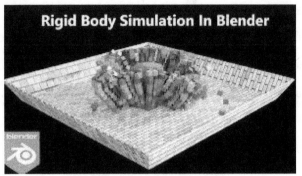

Rigid Body Simulation

2. Rigid Body Fracturing and Destruction

- **New Rigid Body Fracture System**: The newest Blender 4.3 update brings a professional capability for slipping materials between rigid body items. The feature enables users to split rigid body objects into simpler parts without extra work. Some video game developers improve their damage effects through intense object damage simulations to show genuine destruction behavior like real-world cracking responses.

- **Better Control Over Fracture Patterns**: Users gain better fracture control because they now select and shape object breaks after the update added new ways to define fracture patterns. The new simulation tool lets users create realistic material breaks as wood splits and concrete disintegrates while glass shatters in a similar way.

- **Voronoi Fracture Support**: Blender 4.3 delivers new tools for Voronoi fracturing which produces natural breaks across objects and surfaces. This simulation best shows crack development in stone and glass materials plus ice pieces because they naturally fracture at unclear boundaries.

3. Rigid Body Constraints Enhancements

- **Improved Rigid Body Constraints**: The new workflow for rigid body contact now gives users stronger management tools over how separate bodies make contact. The latest Blender 4.3 update allows users to set stricter constraint limits while giving applications more stability through performance enhancements.

- **New Constraint Types**: A new set of restrictions added to the system lets users extend their object control functions and interactive options with system updates. Users benefit from updated hinge and sliding mechanics to do advanced mechanical tests and take full control over object movement.

- **Advanced Spring and Rope Dynamics**: Updated control options represent improved methods to handle spring and rope dynamics connections in the product. The new flexible material system makes ropes chains and elastic bands act realistically as they resist or support direct compressive and tensile forces.

Rigid Body Constraints

4. Bullet Physics Improvements

- **Bullet Physics Engine Optimization**: Blender 4.3 uses improved methods to speed up Bullet physics engine performance especially while simulating large quantities of physical objects and difficult mechanical systems. Better simulation performance reduces task completion time and allows users to edit faster permitting efficient task management.

- **Rigid Body Soft Body Hybrid**: Blender 4.3 allows better interactions between rigid and soft body objects through its better hybrid simulation. The rigid body soft body hybrid system allows for accurate simulations when dealing with objects that mix in stiffness levels such as car wheels on rubber mats or metal items hitting soft materials.

Bullet Physics for Blender

5. Better Support for Soft Body and Cloth Interactions

- **Improved Rigid Body and Soft Body Interactions**: The new contacts improve how rigid and soft materials react. Blender 4.3 creates strong and reliable connections between hard and soft physical objects during contact moments.
- **Cloth and Rigid Body Collisions**: Smoothing materials in Blender 4.3 show accurate results when clothing touches rigid objects. The program controls

cloth reactions accurately during hard surface impacts against soft fabric like a table strike or clothes making contact with body parts.

6. Performance and Stability Enhancements

- **Improved Multithreading for Rigid Body Simulations**: With Blender 4.3 the hardware benefit of using multiple cores during rigid body simulations increased multithreading performance. The new progress boosts speed during entire complex destruction and rigid body processing.

- **Optimized Memory Management**: This update optimizes how Blender 4.3 handles memory use in rigid body simulations which makes it easier to manage many computer objects in the application. Memory use continued to perform well during the new system operations even with big complicated simulation projects.

7. Gravity and Force Field Improvements

- **Advanced Gravity and Force Field Controls**: The new release allows Blender users to better adjust gravity fields and power behaviors of rigid bodies. In Blender 4.3 users gain better controls to regulate the strength and direction of gravity while applying forces from wind, magnetism and electricity that affect object movement.

- **Customizable Force Fields**: In Blender 4.3 users now benefit from adjustable force field controls that let them modify force power levels and specify areas of effectiveness. The added features help users create advanced effects to make objects move in response to nearby wind variations and adjust their behavior in magnetism fields and spatial gravity changes.

8. Rigid Body Caching and Baking Enhancements

- **Faster Baking and Caching**: The rigid body simulation baking received an optimization that decreased the time requirements for simulation processing as well as data caching. After optimization artists now experience faster preview and iteration occasions with rigid body dynamics including destruction and interactions and constraints because simulation results take less waiting time.

- **Persistent Caching**: The stable caching solution in Blender Version 4.3 keeps rigid body simulation data latent across scene changes and file reopening processes. Through this system users can operate on extensive simulated scenes without interruption because it auto-saves calculation results thus eliminating time-consuming complete restarts.

9. Integration with Other Physics Systems

- **Better Integration with Particles and Smoke**: The Blender 4.3 update establishes improved function for rigid body objects to work together with particles and to interact with smoke effects. The enhanced interaction system preserves correct movement between all dynamic elements including explosion-generated debris together with impact-scattered particles and motion-driven smoke movement.

- **Rigid Body and Fluid Interactions**: Tight interconnection exists between fluid and rigid body systems which allows solid elements to react better with liquid elements in their interaction processes. A new system update enables users to rephrase fluid dynamics patterns from water table splashes to liquid debris flow simulation.

10. Interactive Rigid Body Editing

- **On-the-Fly Editing**: Users can edit rigid bodies while their workflow progresses through Blender

4.3 without stopping the operation. Through the running simulation users gain the ability to edit rigid body objects by adjusting constraints and forces together with collision parameters without halting the workflow.

- **Real-Time Feedback**: The real-time visualization of simulated changes undergesistent while Blender 4.3 users modify rigid body simulation parameters because it helps for creating destruction effects within complex multi-part scenes. Summary of Physics and Rigid Body Updates in Blender 4.3:

Summary of Physics and Rigid Body Updates in Blender 4.3:

- Simulations from rigid body perform at faster speeds using optimized solvers and performance optimizers for increased stability.
- A new breaking mechanism based on Voronoi fracturing and improved ability to control pattern destruction routines are included in this application.
- The rigid body constraints received enhancements that enable users to reach superior mechanical simulation precision with better flexibility.

- The software platform allows users to merge rigid body simulation with software body simulation thus creating high-end hybrid simulation abilities.
- Large scene performance improvements occur because of enhanced multithreading while memory optimization leads to accelerated simulation processes.
- There exists a need to build better functionality into the physics system for better interaction among cloth soft bodies and fluids.
- Objects now benefit from superior force field and gravity controls within external conditions because of system improvements.
- Updated features succeed in accelerating both caching operations and baking operations to reduce simulation periods across multiple iterations.
- During real-time simulation operations users can alter interactive simulation parameters through the software interface.

The current system updates deliver increased computational strength to Blender for performing sophisticated and life-like rigid body dynamics and destruction simulations that improve the efficiency of building both tiny and expansive physical scenarios.

CHAPTER SEVEN

GREASE PENCIL

New Drawing and Animation Features

The Blender 4.3 software version includes multiple advanced brush tools in combination with enhanced features that boost workflow efficiency and expand capabilities for 2D and 3D content production. The latest software updates include vital Grease Pencil tools which integrate with drawing features and animation system updates that improve drawing precision and create flexible animation solutions for 2D and 3D applications. Blender 4.3 introduces enhanced drawing and animation features combined with drawing capabilities among its new additions:

1. Grease Pencil Enhancements

- **Sculpt Mode for Grease Pencil**: The latest Blender version 4.3 includes Sculpt Mode for Grease Pencil thus allowing users to handle 2D strokes through 3D sculpting design methods. The animation toolset now provides improved stroke control features to users who need detailed 2D animation through adjustable stroke thickness combined with curvature effects and drawing shape capabilities.

- **Advanced Brush Settings**: The advanced brush settings introduced in Blender 4.3 enable Grease Pencil users to enhance their drawing ability and precision due to new brush settings. The new features enable artists to get better control over their pressure sensitivity adjustments along with stroke jitter commands and texture effects management. Through newly added tools users acquire better abilities to create in-depth 2D artwork alongside animated outputs.

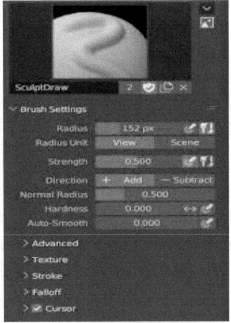

Brush Settings

- **Better Line Art Generation**: The line art generator produces enhanced undetailed outlines that deliver better operational freedom. The new tools aid artists to create refined drawing movements specifically when transforming three-dimensional models into two-dimensional artwork intended for animated stylization purposes.

- **Improved Layer Management**: The latest Blender 4.3 version provides better access to control and organize multiple 2D drawing layers using natural interface systems. The recent software update lets users handle their layers more effectively to boost their animated projects.

Layers

2. New Drawing Tools and Features

- **Enhanced Stroke Editing**: The Blender 4.3 version provides advanced selection functionality to edit strokes during drawings. Through new drawing tools users can edit stroke points as well as refine curved shapes drawn as lines or paths which improves their ability to manage shapes with precision.

- **Improved Smooth Stroke Feature**: Rendered freehand strokes achieved better smoothness thanks to the enhanced implementation of smooth stroke features that deal with tremor effects. The drawing tool assists artists to produce accurate lines either during freehand drawing or executing animation tasks in 2D and 3D artistic spaces.

- **Vector and Raster Brushes**: Artists gain drawing flexibility through new vector and raster brushes that let them produce stylized drawings in addition to photo-realistic illustrations. The user can achieve artistic flexibility by optimizing drawing effects such as sketching and inking and painting with these brushes for various style explorations.

- **Drawing on Meshes**: With the 4.3 Blender update users gained the ability to draw directly on meshes because of the Grease Pencil feature development. Users can create 2D drawings on 3D objects by using this feature which allows them to add style or art in digital three-dimensional environments.

3. Animation System Overhaul

- **Non-Linear Animation (NLA) Improvements**: Non-Linear Animation (NLA) editor received enhanced blend functionality together with multiple-action control as part of its recent improvements. Users gain access to contextual animation setups because they can now blend different animation clips to achieve complex movement controls in both characters and objects.

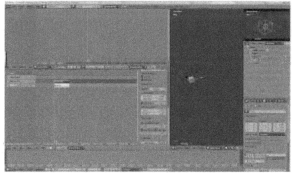

Non – Linear Animation

- **New Animation Layers**: The Blender 4.3 software update brought animation layers to its suite that lets animators divide object and character movements into distinct segments. The animation functionality update grants users enhanced control to modify separate animation components which maintains their complete creative autonomy over finished products.

New Animation Layers

- **Pose Library Updates**: The pose library experienced updates that improved storage for character poses and their related organizational features and application procedures. Better control interfaces and pose management tools in new updates allow animators to generate complex animations that require different character poses.

4. Animation Workflow Enhancements

- **Auto Keyframe Improvements**: Auto Keyframe Improvements in the animation software delivered better control capabilities to users during their movements. Improved animation precision can be achieved by users while setting keyframes because the interface provides more robust features for managing keyframe creation and deletion. The overall animation process speeds up substantially when using this system mainly because of its ability to streamline complex motions made by those who animate difficult scenes and characters.

- **Motion Path Visualization**: The viewport displays animated object motion paths through Motion Path Visualization which Blender 4.3 users can access. When animators view screen-based motion paths they gain better clarity of object motions which enhances their precision during keyframe editing and animation work.

- **Improved Timeline Navigation**: The timeline operation speed received several updates to provide maximum usability for users. Animators can manage large animations easily by using improved scrubbing speed in conjunction with customizable view modes.

5. New Character Animation Tools

- **Better Rigging for Animation**: Users can animate characters with enhanced rigging tools that make animation process quicker and more manageable in Blender 4.3. The new rigging tools bring improved simplicity to automation systems that help users build complex character rig systems and enhance the setup of animated characters for both expert artists and novice beginners.

Better Rigging

- **Customizable Animation Curve Editor**: The new update of Animation Curve Editor in the graph editor enables animators to gain advanced control options for curve manipulation. With keyframe interpolation and timing control animators achieved exact and refined movements when creating either character animations or object motion capabilities.

- **Facial Animation Improvements**: The Blender 4.3 update provides better shape key controls and facial rigging tools to create natural animated facial movements. Animation developers can now use advanced facial expression features to produce authentic facial actions to generate stronger emotional experiences in their animated productions.

6. Grease Pencil and 3D Animation Integration

- **Camera and Depth of Field Control**: The camera function and depth field received improved controls in order to enhance Grease Pencil animation capabilities. Artists benefit from this tool since it enables them to animate 2D drawings whose expanding motions appear realistic through depth simulations that present realistic camera views which smoothly blend with 3D media elements.

- **Grease Pencil and 3D Animation**: Users obtain enhanced control in Blender 4.3 to unite Grease Pencil animations with their 3D models and scenes. The program allows users to build 2D animations directly on 3D models by combining essential features to deliver one adaptable and convenient system for 2D/3D hybrid animation workflows.

Grace Pencil to 3D

7. Improved Keyframe Management

- **Expanded Keyframe Visualization**: The visual representation of keyframes received an update in Blender 4.3 because it enhances both keyframe display abilities and object behavior monitoring. Better animation management and editing becomes possible for animators because extended keyframe visualization reveals enhanced insights about their keyframe effects on object motion and transformations along with deformations.

- **Keyframe Duplication and Offset**: The new Blender 4.3 version helps animators duplicate and offset keyframes which results in simpler and faster

156

replication and motion shifts between timeline areas for various actions. This speeds up the animation process, especially for repetitive motion sequences or character actions.

8. Animation Speed Control and Time Stretching

- **Time Stretching for Animations**: The time stretching feature in Blender 4.3 provides animation users with easy controls to modify animation speed. Through this feature users gain better speed controls for keyframe timings and animation pacing functions during animation clip manipulations in the NLA editor.

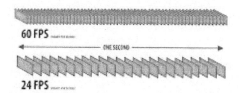

Time Stretching

- **Real-Time Playback Speed Adjustments**: The system enables real-time animation speed adjustments through which users avoid the need for rendering during sequence evaluation and testing processes. This tool enables users to achieve better animation timing refinement by offering increased flexibility through its operation during the analytics stage.

9. 2D and 3D Animation in One Workflow

- **Hybrid 2D/3D Animation**: The new connectivity within Blender 4.3 allows 2D animation elements to combine with 3D animation for single animation production. With its new features Blender enables artists to perform 2D characters animations in 3D space combined with 2D visual enhancement of 3D animation sequences to achieve natural transitions between these animation styles.

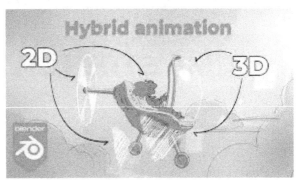

Hybrid 2D/3D Animation

- **Camera Matching for 2D Animation**: The new software capabilities within Blender 4.3 let 2D animators synchronize their animated content to natural camera movements from live-action or 3D visuals. The update provides tools that allow 2D animations to interact smoothly with 3D scenes at 2.5D effect points and when inserting live-action animated elements.

10. Motion Capture and Animation

- **Motion Capture Integration**: The new Blender 4.3 version expands motion capture technology so users can import motion capture files into their 3Drigs after performing effective retargeting operations. The capability improves user workflow by allowing them to animate characters and produce animations at increased speed through realistic human motion data input.

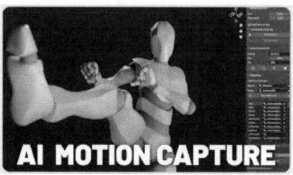

AI Motion Capture

Summary of New Drawing and Animation Features in Blender 4.3:

- The animation file system needs improvement to function efficiently with Grease Pencil sculpting and new drawing brushes combined with advanced layer management capabilities.

- Stroke editing in Blender 4.3 received improvements that resulted in improved drawing performance for both sketching general strokes and precise line work.

- Animation layers and NLA editor improvements for more flexible and dynamic animation setups.

- Better rigging tools for character animation and enhanced pose library functionality.

- Animation users obtain simplified control of timelines as well as better motion paths which enhances their animation editing process.

- The shape key functions of the facial control system delivered superior facial expression outcomes through improved capability improvements.

- The application feature enables users to combine 2D Grease Pencil elements with 3D objects to animate in mixed media settings by using two and three-dimensional parts.

- Children working on animation can use live playback and time stretching capabilities to fully control their animation speed.
- Users can import emotional movements using the upgraded motion capture system to apply them onto three-dimensional animated characters.

The updated drawing and animation features of Blender 4.3 bring enhanced creative options alongside workflow enhancements supported by better user control functionality for 2D and 3D animation features that offer useful tools to professional artists in all sectors.

3D to 2D Workflow Improvements

Multiple updates added in Blender 4.3 make the transition between 3D models and environments with 2D animation more efficient through enhanced features in the 3D to 2D workflow. The updates facilitate automatic transitions between free 3D space capabilities and artistic freedom in 2D animation while maintaining continuous movement between these animation styles. The principal updates included in this section presented themselves as follows:

1. Grease Pencil and 3D Model Integration

- **Drawing on 3D Objects**: The introduction of superior 3D Objects functionality in Blender 4.3 allows artists to make drawings directly on 3D objects through the Grease Pencil tool. The software grants users both capabilities for drawing animated 2D illustrations and making annotations to 3D models. The drawing feature provides artists with the ability to draw 2D sketches that appear directly on top of 3D models surfaces thus facilitating better visual storytelling with combined 3D designs and 2D artwork.

Draw on 3D Object

- **3D Reference for 2D Drawing**: Users now can make 2D drawing animations through 3D model references after this software update. The feature enables developers to merge 3D spaces with 2D characters and objects through proper perspective accuracy for animation projects.

2. Improved Camera Integration

- **2D Animation with 3D Camera Moves**: The new version Blender 4.3 enhances 2D animation production by enabling 3D camera movements as a feature. The latest feature allows artists to animate 2D drawings while their artwork follows 3D camera perspective transformations automatically. Artists use this functionality to blend 2D animated elements with 3D environments which allows them to accomplish dynamic 2D content interactivity within 3D worlds.

Camera Movement

- **Camera Projection for 2D Animation**: The Camera Projection tool enables 2D drawings to appear on 3D surfaces by duplicating traditional 2D drawing styles under control of a 3D camera perspective. Artists today can display their 2D animations with precise depth and perspective matching within 3D spaces through this capability.

3. Grease Pencil in 3D Space

- **Layered 2D Drawing with 3D Interaction**: Users can now generate various Grease Pencil drawings across distinct layers where the drawing layers move with 3D objects yet maintain separate animation controls for each layer.

- **3D Grease Pencil Tools**: 3D Grease Pencil Tools: Blender 4.3 offers enhanced 3D Grease Pencil tools for drawing 2D animations in a fully 3D environment. Users have control over animating 2D elements that follow 3D object paths and they also control how 2D animations can interact with 3D cameras. Users can completely control and place 2D elements and animations within the scene by adjusting 2D strokes through 3D space using the 3D workspace.

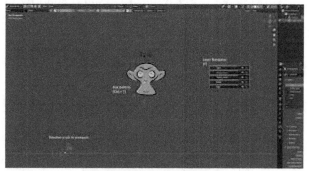

Grease Pencil Tools

4. Hybrid 2D/3D Animation Workflow

- **2D Animation on 3D Objects**: Blender version 4.3 enhances 2D Grease Pencil animation capabilities which allow their users to merge pencil animations with 3D objects. People can preserve their 2D drawing tasks on 3D models while the animated elements generate reactions to the changes in the 3D scene environment. Project 4.3 offers a segmented animation approach that unifies 3D model structures with 2D animation programming.

- **Combining 2D and 3D Effects**: The system now lets users swiftly intermix 2D along with 3D effect applications in their projects. In front of 3D backgrounds a 2D character will keep its precise dimensional depth yet remain fully capable of working with 3D light effects and shadow elements and camera perspectives.

5. Grease Pencil Stroke Refinements

- **Sculpting Grease Pencil Strokes in 3D**: The new 3D tools allow artists to improve their 2D drawings by converting them into editable 3D modelable strokes through Grease Pencil sculpting capabilities. Users can now perform real-time editing of strokes while working between two and three dimensions using three-dimensional objects in a manner similar to typical three-dimensional objects. This tool makes adaptation of 2D artwork in challenging 3D scenes much easier for animators.

- **Automatic Stroke Alignment**: Blender 4.3 features an automatic stroke alignment tool which ensures proper placement of 2D strokes together with their animations when displayed above 3D models or scenes. This tool increases animation precision on 3D objects and improves both speed and usability in the production process.

6. Hybrid Lighting and Shadowing for 2D Elements

- **Lighting 2D Animation with 3D Lighting**: Through Blender 4.3 the software allows integration of 3D lighting with 2D animations which enables the use of 3D illumination techniques for 2D animation elements. The enhanced feature interconnects Grease Pencil 2D drawings and 3D lighting mechanisms for dynamic real-time generation of shadows and highlight effects that modify with 3D lighting fluctuations.

- **Grease Pencil Shadow Casting**: Grease Pencil Shadow Casting introduces an option that produces shadows made through Grease Pencil stroke manipulation which can adhere to 3D objects in the scene thus reinforcing 2D-3D visual coherence.

7. Simplified Workflow for 2D/3D Camera Transitions

- **2D to 3D Camera Matching**: Blender 4.3 provides an enhancement called 2D to 3D Camera Matching that enables straightforward exchange between multiple camera viewpoints within the workspace. The feature grants animators unrestricted access to shift between 2D animation and 3D perspective without affecting camera positions when working on multiple changes. Blender 4.3 offers its artists a valuable tool to combine 2D drawings with 3D work and create 2.5D effects showing flat characters floating in three-dimensional space.

Camera Matching

- **Real-Time Camera and Object Integration**: Artist abilities to track 2D elements and 3D objects and camera movements simultaneously become real-time through this feature while objects stay

168

properly positioned to the scene. The new tool allows users to adjust both 3D objects instantly and 2D animations together which reduces different content editing durations.

8. Improved Export Options for 2D/3D Projects

- **2D/3D Hybrid Rendering**: The Blender 4.3 software enhances its rendering capabilities through new features that enable users to export single projects featuring 2D and 3D visual elements united in a single file. The software lets users merge 2D and 3D elements using a seamless rendering method that enables them to complete 2D/3D animated projects with distinctive visual effects.

- **Exporting 2D and 3D in Separate Layers**: Artists gain superior compositing features from new functionality that enables exporting 2D Grease Pencil animations and 3D models in individual separate layers. Severe post-production work becomes more feasible because these two animation styles can be separated.

9. Enhanced NLA (Non-Linear Animation) for 2D/3D Blending

- **Blending 2D and 3D Animations**: Blender 4.3 introduced upgraded features to the NLA editor which allowed users to blend animations made from 2D Grease Pencil artwork with 3D objects seamlessly. The NLA editor provides tools to handle the interactive sequences of 2D and 3D animation clips that exist in one single timeline.

Blending Animations

- **Layered 2D and 3D Animation**: The integration of 2D animation layers on top of 3D animation enables animators to maintain better coherence between various animation elements in their design.

10. Performance Improvements for 2D/3D Workflows

- **Optimized Performance for Hybrid Animation**: The new Blender 4.3 version offers optimization tools to enhance performance during hybrid animation tasks specifically in cases that mix 2D and 3D animation elements. Workplace artists utilizing Blender 4.3 receive performance improvements through the combination of 2D and 3D elements during their project development and while creating advanced animations that contain massive data quantities.

Summary of 3D to 2D Workflow Improvements in Blender 4.3:

- Grease Pencil drawing directly on 3D objects for more seamless integration of 2D elements in 3D space.
- Improved camera and 3D environment interactions with 2D animation for more dynamic and immersive results.
- The update enables users to create superior solutions that merge 2D character animations with 3D objects and scenes.
- The new software made possible a better technique to integrate lighting and shadows across 2D

animations with 3D lighting environments for achieving consistent visual flow.

- A new real-time camera matching system functions with upgraded camera transition features to provide seamless movement between 2D and 3D picture areas.
- The updated export features let producers distribute their complete 2D and 3D projects from one project through layered animation rendering.
- Hybrid 2D/3D workflows in Blender enable numerous users to work more efficiently with complicated multi-faceted scenes.

The Blender software's version 4.3 brings upgraded workflows that reduces the complexity of uniting different artistic elements across 2D and 3D domains for exceptional animation composition.

CHAPTER NINE

CONCLUSION

What's Next for Blender

The program Blender gained new functions that made it stronger during each product update. The coming releases of Blender will add new functions to match present trends and growth priorities. As development progresses toward the release date multiple new features will be shown to us but these future enhancements seem to follow three main directions:

1. Enhanced Real-Time Rendering and GPU Support

- **Eevee and Cycles Improvements**: The developers will advance both Eevee and Cycles because Eevee demonstrated notable improvements already. The next Eevee updates will enhance reflective performance and bring advanced global illumination methods plus state-of-the-art post-processing techniques to reach Cycles quality levels. The upcoming release will make Cycles X faster and improve its ray tracing and denoising functions.

- **Real-Time Ray Tracing**: By exploiting GPU growth Blender will enable real-time ray tracing that maintains visual quality and offers exact caustic and refractive effects without slowing the workflow.

2. Procedural Generation and Node-Based Workflows

- **Expanded Geometry Nodes**: The subtractive part of Geometry Nodes will grow its procedural tools with further development. The next product updates will introduce complex Geometry Nodes to control object animation and rigging while adding simulation functions to the program. The update will bring deeper procedural generation tools into use by adding performance-optimized features to model making and texture and animation programming. The system needs better ways for users to work together between shader and simulation components while they design in real time.

- **More Procedural Tools**: As procedure tools for Blender evolve they will include model generation with additional texturing and animation features. Integrated procedural tools in Blender will transform artistic modeling systems by giving users enhanced freedom without breaking their work process.

3. AI and Machine Learning Integration

- **AI-Assisted Tools**: New Blender versions will bring AI-based assistance tools that use AI and Machine Learning systems. The current software includes automatic optimization tools alongside self-determining UV unwrapper features together with a predictive lighting composition system that boosts user experience. The AI denoising of Blender helps solve current issues but future updates will let users transmit animation re-targeting and scene configuration while generating textures.

- **AI for Animation**: AI produces natural animations that switch between 2D and 3D positions with automated movements and boosts motion capture results.

4. Better Collaboration and Cloud Integration

- **Cloud-Based Collaboration**: The team at Blender can connect users to work together in the cloud since cloud computing lets them create shared project options. Users can partner live and edit projects with version control through Blender Cloud. Blender would better support remote workgroups when it adds full cloud service synchronization features.

- **Cloud Rendering**: By adding Cloud Rendering features to upcoming Blender updates users will perform big rendering tasks within the application without external tools. The feature would enter the Blender workspace right after its initial launch through enhanced user-interface options.

5. Sculpting and Texturing Enhancements

- **Advanced Sculpting Tools**: Blender's sculpting technology continues to advance and will receive new shaping tools plus dynamic mesh optimization technology besides adding the ability to sculpt between different mesh resolutions. The mix of adaptive subdivision and enhanced brushes and symmetry tools will make Blender work easier for artists.

- **Texture Painting and UV Mapping**: The texture painting and UV mapping tools in software will become better by upgrading highly refined painting tools and giving them more speed and higher accuracy. The methodology behind how artists handle big models in UV unwrapping and packing should perform better to help them work faster.

6. Animation System Advancements

- **Non-Linear Animation (NLA) System Improvements**: Through better NLA System upgrades Blender can improve how users switch between animation states and add more animation features to the timeline. The system updates enhance how animators plan and modify their work process.

- **Faster Rigging and Skinning**: Blender will automate skinning tasks better by refining automatic skinning technology and faster integrating FK and IK systems with improved rigging simplification. Weight painting needs better optimization to speed up times when artists must modify weights several times.

- **Motion Capture Integration**: Blender will let users add mocap data more easily through its new motion capture integration. Blender users will gain better custom rig building tools plus stronger capabilities to transfer animations between different skeleton setups.

7. Virtual Reality (VR) and Augmented Reality (AR)

- **VR/AR Support**: Only increasing use of VR/AR will push Blender developers to improve their VR and AR functions. An improved Blender release will permit users to experience modeling in VR space and preview their work within AR environments. This upcoming tool will create superior design and testing possibilities.

- **VR Sculpting and Modeling**: By making specialized VR modeling tools designers will gain access to new ways of interacting with their work that cannot be done through normal screen displays.

8. Improved Simulations

- **Cloth, Fluid, and Smoke Simulations**: The development of simulation technology will focus on creating better systems that model cloth materials fluid movement and how smoke behaves. The market will progress through better fluids handling software as well as upgraded resources to simulate complex cloth behaviors and tame fire and smoke effects.

- **Rigid Body Physics Enhancements**: The system needs better tools to tear objects and should handle better collisions between hard and soft physical bodies.

9. Asset Management and Marketplace Integration

- **Built-in Asset Library**: The future Blender release will include an Asset Library to make asset management easier and offer straightaway sharing options for users across projects. Through its marketplace Blender will let creators both buy and sell 3D assets bundled with materials and plugins.

- **Improved Asset Browser**: The Asset Browser requires updates that enhance its tagging options and increases project search performance across all projects. Better ways to manage assets would help artists work faster particularly when handling significant projects and big asset collections.

10. Python API and Scripting Enhancements

- **Expanded Python API**: Python API and its capabilities will grow as Blender receives more updates. After factory testing Blender will provide increased Geometry Nodes support and Window Design choices in their new updates. With a better Python API interface both scripters and developers can fully manage automated work processes and develop powerful Blender tools.

- **Customizable Workspaces and UI**: Users can design and adjust their work space features plus user interface elements for their personal work needs. Users must have a simple method to move graphics features within the interface and produce reusable UI designs.

11. Cross-Platform and Interoperability Improvements

- **Better Integration with External Tools**: Blender will connect easier to Autodesk Maya and similar programs through future updates as part of its expansion options. The program will add new import/export tools along with more file type support and faster movement between diverse digital tools.

- **Cloud and Web-Based Tools**: Blender tools based in the cloud will develop further for users who need software system access on weaker computers and efficient collaboration functions. The Blender interface will get more benefits from cloud solutions by providing online tools plus cloud-hosted simulation computers.

12. Better Education and Documentation

- **Enhanced Documentation**: The available Blender guidance materials will receive improved updates to assist everyone from beginners to experts in using the software system.

- **Integrated Learning Resources**: The proposed system merges teaching resources inside the Blender application screen to teach new users in one integrated program.

Conclusion

Blender stands strong in its path ahead as developers improve all parts of the software including improved simulations better teamwork elements and advanced AI technology. The Blender open-source project expands boundaries each day to create software that works better for users. Through its position between design development and animation Blender shows strong signs of continued innovation that will maintain its position as popular software in 3D creation during the next few years.

www.ingramcontent.com/pod-product-compliance
Lightning Source LLC
La Vergne TN
LVHW022345060326
832902LV00022B/4259